PROGRAMME
THEOLOGY FOR TODAY

MODULE

THE PAULINE WRITINGS

UNITS FOUR, FIVE, SIX AND SEVEN

**THE
PRIORY
INSTITUTE**

THE PAULINE WRITINGS

THE PRIORY INSTITUTE

The Priory Institute, established in the Dominican tradition, is a centre for education in theological and biblical studies. It offers an extensive range of seminars and programmes including an accredited certificate, diploma and degree in theology by distance learning.

THE PRIORY INSTITUTE TEAM

Joseph Kavanagh *moderator*
John Littleton *head of distance education*
Martin Cogan *general editor*
Joseph Cullen *tutor support*
Teresa Proudfoot *student services administrator*

THEOLOGY FOR TODAY

Level One: (certificate programme)

1. Introduction to Theology
2. Introduction to Scripture
3. Introduction to Philosophy
4. Introduction to Christian Spirituality

Levels Two and Three: (diploma and degree programmes)

5. Fundamental Theology
6. Themes in Modern Philosophy
7. The God of Christian Faith
8. Fundamental Moral Theology
9. Church History
10. Christianity and World Religions
11. The Gospel of Mark
12. A Just Society?
13. Isaiah and Biblical Prophecy
14. Philosophical Theology
15. Trinity & Incarnate Word
16. Caring for Life
17. Soteriology and Eschatology
18. The Psalms
19. The Church Gathered and Gathering
20. The Pauline Writings

THE PAULINE WRITINGS

Series:	Theology for Today
Series Number:	Twenty
Title:	The Pauline Writings Volume Two
Contents:	Unit Four: The Letter to Philemon
	Unit Five: First and Second Letters to the Corinthians
	Unit Six: The Letter to the Philippians
	Unit Seven: The Letter to the Romans
	Module Conclusions
ISBN:	978-1-905193-61-5
Author:	Kieran J. O'Mahony
Published by:	The Priory Institute
Editors:	Martin Cogan and John Littleton
Typesetting:	The Priory Institute
Design:	The Priory Institute
Printing:	Glennon & Company, Ashbourne Business Park, Ashbourne, Co Meath, Ireland

The Priory Institute
Tallaght Village, Dublin 24, Ireland
Telephone: (+353-1) 404 8124. Fax: (+353-1) 462 6084
email: enquiries@prioryinstitute.com   Website: www.prioryinstitute.com

THE PAULINE WRITINGS
MODULE CONTENTS

CONTENTS

THE PAULINE WRITINGS:
UNITS FOUR, FIVE, SIX AND SEVEN

UNIT SIX: THE LETTER TO THE PHILIPPIANS

UNIT SEVEN: THE LETTER TO THE ROMANS

THE PAULINE WRITINGS

PROGRAMME
THEOLOGY FOR TODAY

MODULE
THE PAULINE WRITINGS

UNIT FOUR
THE LETTER TO PHILEMON

UNIT INTRODUCTION

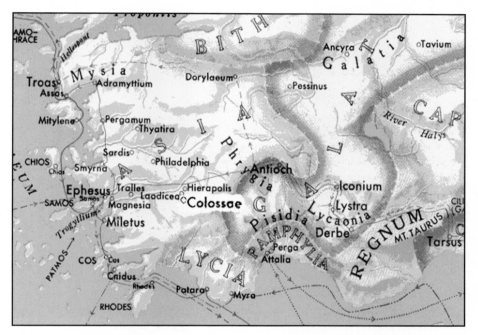

Fig. 1: *Paths followed by Paul*

I. PERSONAL, BUT NOT PRIVATE

The shortest letter of St Paul is his *Letter to Philemon*. It will serve as a reminder both of letter-writing and rhetoric, as well as provide a window on the social world of the Pauline mission. The letter has been much studied in recent decades in an attempt to resolve the puzzles which are present in even so short a text. It was not always a magnet for scholars because of its lack of theological argument. The letter is personal, although not really private. One can hear the voice of Paul in a different key.

 Task

a) *Read the* Letter to Philemon, *and wonder about it.*

2. LEARNING OUTCOMES

By the end of this unit, students will have learned about:

a) The context and setting of *Philemon*;

b) The use of letter-writing and speech analysis;

c) A more personal side of Paul; and

d) Slavery as a part of society at the time.

SECTION ONE:
THE STYLE OF ST PAUL

Fig. 2: *Paul, Apphia and Philemon*

I.   PHILEMON IN THE PAULINE CORPUS

The Pauline authorship of the *Letter to Philemon* has never been seriously questioned. People did wonder, in the fourth and fifth centuries, why so slight a text should be part of the Bible. Later, in the nineteenth century, some scholars thought the work novelistic and unreal, and so hardly genuinely from Paul. In these approaches, the presuppositions are as interesting as the results!

It has been shown from its vocabulary alone (and indeed from its rhetoric) that the letter is indeed genuinely from Paul. The form used for 'Jesus Christ' is in the reverse order – 'Christ Jesus' – and is typically Pauline, and is found in *Philemon* verses 1 and 9. Other typically Pauline expressions are 'co-worker' (Phlm 1,24), 'in the Lord' (Phlm 16,20) and the phrase 'to say nothing of' (Phlm 19).

What context can we imagine for this short document and what history lies behind it? To answer this question, It may help to begin with the *dramatis personae*.

- Paul – who is in prison;
- Timothy, Paul's fellow worker;
- Philemon, the leader of a house church;
- Onesimus, a slave, mentioned also in Colossians 4:9; the name means 'profitable', giving rise to a pun in the letter;
- Archippus, also mentioned in Colossians 4:17;
- Apphia, a woman, not mentioned elsewhere; and
- five other who append greetings to the *Letter*: Epaphras, Mark, Aristarchus, Demas and Luke.

1.1   ALL AS IT SEEMS?

Many questions need answering:

- Where was Paul at this time?
- When was the letter written?
- Was Onesimus actually a runaway slave?
- Was Paul the good Roman citizen, returning him to his owner?
- Are there other possibilities within the social context?
- How was it that this slight letter survived and found its way into the New Testament?

It is impossible to answer many of these questions, and others can only get a probable answer. It seems probable that Philemon's house church may very well have been in Colossae, given that Archippus and Onesimus lived there. It could be that Apphia was the wife of Philemon and Archippus a family member, perhaps his son.

The traditional reading was that Paul was in Rome at this stage. This is perhaps unlikely because he hoped to make a return visit, which seems impossible because Paul's purpose in being in Rome was to go on from there to Spain. Different locations have been proposed, but the most probable place for the writing of the letter is Ephesus, from where it would have been very easy to get to Colossae. There is no mention in *Acts* of an imprisonment in Ephesus, but it is not impossible (see 1 Cor 15:32; 2 Cor 1:8-11).

Perhaps the most plausible reconstruction is also the least dramatic. It was not unknown for slaves to run away, not necessarily to escape permanently but to find a friend of the owner so as to negotiate better conditions. This would explain why a slave 'ran away' to a prominent friend. It would also account for the tone and content of the letter. In the course of his time with Paul, Onesimus fell under the influence of the apostle and converted to Christianity. In the letter, Paul does not hesitate to use this fact to encourage Philemon to be extra generous, not only because of Paul but because Onesimus was now a brother in the Lord.

2.   PHILEMON AS A LETTER AND A SPEECH

As a letter, *Philemon* is the one Pauline document which really resembles a typical Hellenistic letter. It is short and shows all the features of such a letter. At the same time, it breathes a powerful air of compact persuasion and it is no surprise to learn that it can also be analysed using the structure of rhetoric.

Verses	Letter	Speech	Content
1-3	Superscript		Senders, recipient, greetings
4-7	Thanksgiving	Introduction	Praise for Philemon's faith and love
8-22	Body	Proof (8-16)	Appeal on behalf of Onesimus
		Conclusion (17-22)	Amplification of the appeal
23-25	Postscript		Greetings from five others

The commentary below will show how the different parts function in this letter. But before that, there is one further peculiarity. It is possible to make a chiastic reading of the letter, along the lines of ABBA. This is best seen by observing the text itself.

Phlm 1: Paul, a prisoner of Christ Jesus, and Timothy our brother, to Philemon our dear friend and co-worker, ²to Apphia our sister, to Archippus our fellow soldier, and to the church in your house: ³Grace to you and peace from God our Father and the Lord Jesus Christ.	*Names, fellow-workers, greetings*	**Phlm 23:** Epaphras, my fellow prisoner in Christ Jesus, sends greetings to you, ²⁴and so do Mark, Aristarchus, Demas, and Luke, my fellow workers. ²⁵The grace of the Lord Jesus Christ be with your spirit.
4: When I remember you in my prayers, I always thank my God ⁵because I hear of your love for all the saints and your faith toward the Lord Jesus.	*Paul and Philemon pray for each other*	**22:** One thing more – prepare a guest room for me, for I am hoping through your prayers to be restored to you.
6: I pray that the sharing of your faith may become effective when you perceive all the good that we may do for Christ.	*Paul's confidence in Philemon*	**21:** Confident of your obedience, I am writing to you, knowing that you will do even more than I say.
7: I have indeed received much joy and encouragement from your love, because the hearts of the saints have been refreshed through you, my brother.	*Refreshment of heart*	**20:** Yes, brother, let me have this benefit from you in the Lord! Refresh my heart in Christ.
8: For this reason, though I am bold enough in Christ to command you to do your duty, ⁹yet I would rather appeal to you on the basis of love – and I, Paul, do this as an old man, and now also as a prisoner of Christ Jesus.	*Paul could command but prefers to appeal*	**19:** I, Paul, am writing this with my own hand: I will repay it. I say nothing about your owing me even your own self.
10: I am appealing to you for my child, Onesimus, whose father I have become during my imprisonment. ¹¹Formerly he was useless to you, but now he is indeed useful both to you and to me.	*The "useless" Onesimus has become useful*	**18:** If he has wronged you in any way, or owes you anything, charge that to my account.
12: I am sending him, that is, my own heart, back to you.	*Paul wants Philemon to treat Onesimus as if he were treating Paul*	**17:** So if you consider me your partner, welcome him as you would welcome me.
13: I wanted to keep him with me, so that he might be of service to me in your place during my imprisonment for the gospel; ¹⁴but I preferred to do nothing without your consent, in order that your good deed might be voluntary and not something forced.	*Onesimus now a brother could be very useful to Paul*	**15:** Perhaps this is the reason he was separated from you for a while, so that you might have him back forever, ¹⁶no longer as a slave but more than a slave, a beloved brother – especially to me but how much more to you, both in the flesh and in the Lord.

The apparent simplicity of the letter is only a surface observation. In reality, this carefully written appeal, following all the rules of letter-writing and rhetoric, is also in its own way most artistically composed.

EXERCISE 1:

a) *What is the setting of the* Letter to Philemon *in the life of Paul? Write 5 lines.*

b) *What are the literary features of the* Letter to Philemon? *Write 5 lines.*

3. COMMENTARY

3.1 PHILEMON 1-3: SUPERSCRIPT

¹Paul, a prisoner of Christ Jesus, and Timothy our brother, to Philemon our dear friend and co-worker, ²to Apphia our sister, to Archippus our fellow soldier, and to the church in your house: ³Grace to you and peace from God our Father and the Lord Jesus Christ. (Phlm 1:1-3)

The superscript is warm and personal. If Apphia and Archippus are indeed the wife and son of Philemon, the passage enjoys even more effectiveness.

3.2 PHILEMON 4-7: THANKSGIVING / INTRODUCTION

Fig. 3: *Apphia and Archippus*

⁴When I remember you in my prayers, I always thank my God ⁵because I hear of your love for all the saints and your faith toward the Lord Jesus. ⁶I pray that the sharing of your faith may become effective when you perceive all the good that we may do for Christ. ⁷I have indeed received much joy and encouragement from your love, because the hearts of the saints have been refreshed through you, my brother. (Phlm 4-7)

These verses fulfill the function of the thanksgiving in all Paul's letters, with the exception of *Galatians*. As an introduction, it achieves the three aims of the introduction:

a) to win the attention of the hearers;
b) to get their good will; and
c) to make them receptive to the speaker.

Attention and good will are gained by telling Philemon he prays for him. A good feeling towards Paul will be engendered by Paul's own experience of joy, encouragement and love through Philemon.

3.3 PHILEMON 8-16: APPEAL ON BEHALF OF ONESIMUS

⁸For this reason, though I am bold enough in Christ to command you to do your duty, ⁹yet I would rather appeal to you on the basis of love – and I, Paul, do this as an old man, and now also as a prisoner of Christ Jesus. ¹⁰I am appealing to you for my child, Onesimus, whose father I have become during my imprisonment. ¹¹Formerly he was useless to you, but now he is indeed useful both to you and to me. ¹²I am sending him, that is, my own heart, back to you. ¹³I wanted to keep him with me, so that he might be of service to me in your place during my imprisonment for the gospel; ¹⁴but I preferred to do nothing without your consent, in order that your good deed might be voluntary and not something forced. ¹⁵Perhaps this is the reason he was separated from you for a while, so that you might have him back forever, ¹⁶no longer as a slave but more than a slave, a beloved brother – especially to me but how much more to you, both in the flesh and in the Lord. (Phlm 1:8-16)

The thesis is really found in verse 10 which states plainly what the letter is about. That clear statement is preceded by a typical *captatio benevolentiae*, a gaining of good will again. This is achieved:

a)   by foregoing the right to command; preferring instead to appeal on the basis of love; and

b)   by mentioning Paul's age and condition as a prisoner.

Each verse is a powerful appeal.

v.11:   a play on the name Onesimus, which means useful;

v.12:   a highly emotional sending – he now represents Paul himself;

v.13:   in Paul's mind, Onesimus represented Philemon himself;

v.14:   Paul prefers free consent to force; and

vv.15-16:   a kind reading of the escape, in the light of Onesimus' conversion.

3.4   PHILEMON 17-22: AMPLIFICATION OF THE APPEAL

> [17]So if you consider me your partner, welcome him as you would welcome me. [18]If he has wronged you in any way, or owes you anything, charge that to my account. [19]I, Paul, am writing this with my own hand: I will repay it. I say nothing about your owing me even your own self. [20]Yes, brother, let me have this benefit from you in the Lord! Refresh my heart in Christ. [21]Confident of your obedience, I am writing to you, knowing that you will do even more than I say. [22]One thing more – prepare a guest room for me, for I am hoping through your prayers to be restored to you. (Phlm 17-22)

This section fulfills very well the function of a conclusion, or *peroratio*. The purpose of this part of a speech was to summarise, to appeal to the emotions and to amplify slightly the reasons for the appeal. All are present here.

peroratio

v.17:   a repetition of verse 10, the thesis;

v.18:   amplification by anticipating any objection on financial grounds;

v.19:   apparently passing Philemon's debt to Paul;

v.20:   a direct and emotional appeal;

v.21:   a return to the praise offered at the start of the letter; and

v.22:   an appeal for prayer that Paul may be released and come to Philemon. It is implied that Paul will thus be able to check on Philemon.

3.5   PHILEMON 23-25: POSTSCRIPT

> [23]Epaphras, my fellow prisoner in Christ Jesus, sends greetings to you, [24]and so do Mark, Aristarchus, Demas, and Luke, my fellow workers. [25]The grace of the Lord Jesus Christ be with your spirit. (Phlm 23-25)

The letter closes on a quite personal note, with greetings from many others. This has the effect of making the letter rather more public, and of making Philemon's response likewise rather more public.

EXERCISE 2:

a)   Who are the personalities mentioned in the Letter to Philemon? Write 5 lines.

b)   What was Paul's attitude to slavery in the letter? Write 5 lines.

UNIT FOUR CONCLUSIONS

I. CONCLUSION

This short letter is a reminder of Paul's immense powers of persuasion, his original adaptation of the letter structure, his subtle use of rhetorical devices and the sheer artistry of his writings. One can also see in *Philemon* a very human, very warm side to Paul the old man, and now a prisoner.

Today, of course, the question is asked, What was Paul's attitude to slavery? Slavery in those days exhibited a range of conditions – from unfortunate, chained miners to highly educated tutors. Often an attachment grew up between the owner and the slave, so that owners gave their most beloved slaves their freedom – before their death or in their wills. It must frankly be said that Paul did not take on or criticise the institution of slavery at that time. However, the reality of Onesimus' becoming a Christian makes the old relationship to his owner no longer applicable. In that sense, *Philemon* is a practical illustration of what Paul said in *Galatians*,

Paul did not criticise the institution of slavery.

> As many of you as were baptised into Christ have clothed yourselves with Christ. There is no longer Jew or Greek, there is no longer slave or free, there is no longer male and female; for all of you are one in Christ Jesus. And if you belong to Christ, then you are Abraham's offspring, heirs according to the promise. (Gal 3:27–29)

2. LEARNING OUTCOMES ASSESSED

By the end of this short unit, in addition to the learning outcomes listed at the start of the unit, students should:

a) be aware of how the rhetorical devices outlined in earlier units apply; and

b) know about the different, rather more personal, dimension to Paul.

PROGRAMME
THEOLOGY FOR TODAY

MODULE
THE PAULINE WRITINGS

UNIT FIVE
THE LETTERS TO THE CORINTHIANS

INTRODUCTION TO UNIT FIVE

I.   QUESTIONS ON *CORINTHIANS*

This unit on Paul's correspondence with the Corinthians covers both 1 *and* 2 *Corinthians*. As these letters cover a wide variety of material, not every verse is analysed in the detail that was done for the Thessalonian correspondence earlier in this module.

The unit covers the social, political and geographical features of the city of Corinth, and then goes on to examine the structure and content of 1 *Corinthians*. Only selected passages from 1 *and* 2 *Corinthians* are examined in detail.

Of special interest for theologians and Scripture scholars alike is the text of the Lord's Supper. This is the earliest description of the Christian assembly found in the New Testament, and its importance cannot be overestimated. The fascinating thing is that the very chaotic nature of the multicultural Christian community in Corinth gave rise to considerable problems, and it was in addressing these very problems that St Paul has given us a sort of window into the life of the early Church, both the good sides and the troublesome features.

As always in this module, it is the rhetorical devises which provide the key to unlock the structure and theological content of the letters.

Task

a) Before reading one of the letters of St Paul, it is possible to set out a number of questions which can guide one's interpretation and analysis. Read the two Corinthian letters now.

2. LEARNING OUTCOMES

By the end of this unit, students should have a thorough knowledge of:

a) the setting of the Corinthian correspondence, with special attention to:

    i.   the history and archaeology of Corinth, and

    ii.   the membership of the Corinthian churches;

b) the occasion and structure of 1 *Corinthians*;

c) Paul's theology of the cross (1 Cor 1-4).

d) the practice of the Lord's Supper (1 Cor 11);

e) the role of spiritual gifts (1 Cor 12-14);

f) Paul's understanding of the resurrection (1 Cor 15);

g) the occasion and structure of 2 *Corinthians* 8-9; and

h) the theology behind the Jerusalem collection.

SECTION ONE:
THE CITY OF CORINTH

Fig. 4: *Corinth at the Crossroads*

1.   CORINTH

Ancient Corinth has sometimes been compared with modern Las Vegas: a flashy city, a febrile society, financial mobility and, as in all caricatures, there is something of an exaggeration. But as the differences are greater than the similarities, this unit attempts to build a more accurate image of the ancient city and its inhabitants.[1] It is, in effect, an exercise in historical imagination. Two central questions will be asked:

*   What was Roman Corinth like?

*   Who were the Christian Corinthians?

1.1   WHAT WAS ROMAN CORINTH LIKE?

The Greek city of Corinth, as distinct from the later Roman foundation, was legendary for its beauty. So much so, that when the Greek city was destroyed, several very touching 'epitaphs' were written. Livy wrote:

> This city before its destruction was a place of outstanding beauty; its citadel, within the walls, rising up to an immense height, abounding in springs of water, while the Isthmus separated by this narrow passage two neighbouring seas to the east and west.
>
> (Murphy-O'Connor, Jerome: *St Paul's Corinth*, p.75)

---

1.   This essay is the adaptation of a paper given at an IBA conference, *The Church in the New Testament* in 1996. To people familiar with the literature, it will be clear how much this text is indebted to other authors; this can be seen, not only in the few footnotes but also in the bibliography. .

The beauty of Corinth reflected its wealth and, in turn, its wealth depended on its location. Corinth – in the isthmus leading from Athens to the southern part of Achaia – controlled the isthmus, and from that derived much of the importance of Corinth. Corinth had two natural ports:

Lechaion
Cenchreae

- Cenchreae, on the eastern side of the isthmus; and
- Lechaion on the western side.

Depending on the time of year, the weather south of the peninsula made it dangerous to travel by sea and it was both cheaper and safer to go overland from Cenchreae through Corinth to Lechaion. Cenchreae was the smaller port, but it has been excavated. Lechaion, one of the largest man-made harbours in antiquity, has not been excavated. Trade there was international, coming not only from all over the Mediterranean, but also from India, China and even Indonesia.[2] Approaching the city from Lechaion, a visitor would see a very cosmopolitan city, full of businessmen, tourists, pilgrims, farmers and merchants.

On the road south-east from Lechaion towards Corinth, visitors would be struck by height of the Acrocorinth 'behind' the city. On top, there was a temple to Aphrodite – because Corinth was dedicated to the Greek version of the Roman Venus.

Aphrodite

The city enjoyed all the facilities of a prosperous Greco-Roman town: colonnaded walks, gymnasia, fountains, bath houses, public latrines, swimming pools, beautiful basilicas, impressive temples, public monuments and works of art. In particular, the water in Corinth was both abundant and safe, thanks to the numerous springs around the city. The visitor's first impression has been summarised enthusiastically by Engels:

> The forum itself was a vast, open space thronged with merchants, street-hawkers, travellers and local residents. Vari-colored tents covered the market stalls. Surveying the scene, he would see important works of pubic art: paintings, marble sculpture, and works of bronze by renowned artists. The Forum was the religious as well as commercial core of the city, and contained numerous shrines, sanctuaries, and temples, the greatest of which was the Archaic Temple, perhaps dedicated to Corinth's founding dynasty, the Gens Julia. Surrounding the Forum were the temples, shops, stoas, and the administrative offices in the imposing South Stoa … What would strike our visitor most was the dazzling colors, white marbles and marble stuccoes, and the astonishing variety of polychrome marble revetment with which many of the buildings were covered: blues, violets, greens, reds and yellows in every conceivable combination. And now he would have been convinced that he had indeed entered the Aphrodite of cities, the promenade of Hellas, the shining light of Greece.
>
> (Engels, Donald: *Roman Corinth – An Alternative Model for the Classical City*, 1990, Chicago-London, The University of Chicago Press, p.13f)

EXERCISE 1:

a) *What was the geographical location of Corinth? Write 5 lines.*

b) *What was the appearance of the Greco-Roman city? Write 5 lines.*

---

2.   Engels: *Roman Corinth* p.12.

2. HISTORY OF CORINTH

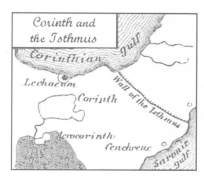

Behind the reassurance of such opulent prosperity lay a turbulent history which falls into two periods. The first is the history of the Greek city, up to 146 bce (that year, the city was destroyed by the Romans and the inhabitants sent into exile). And from 146 bce until 46 bce when Corinth was re-founded as a Roman Colony. In between, Corinth was effectively, though perhaps not completely, abandoned.

The destruction of the Greek city of Corinth followed a series of wars and alliances which culminated in the Roman siege of 146 bce. Prior to that, Corinth had nimbly switched between Macedonian control and the Achaian League. This mobility clashed with the stolidity of the Romans, and when, after a series of calculated insults to official envoys, the Romans declared war, the writing was on the wall. A better trained and numerically superior Roman army annihilated the defenders of Greece at the battle of Leucopetra in 146 bce. The already abandoned and eerie Corinth was taken and burned. Women and children were sold into slavery, and the men put to death.[3]

Battle of Leucopetra

Following that defeat, the Romans allowed other cites to be rebuilt – except Corinth, which became legally an *ager Romanus* and was farmed for the Roman government by the Sikyonians. Cicero visited the ruins, probably between 79 and 77 bce and he wrote:

> The sudden sight of the ruins of Corinth had more effect on me than the actual inhabitants; for long contemplation[4] had a hardening effect on their souls.
>
> (Engels: *Roman Corinth*, p.15)

Just before his death, Julius Caesar (100-44 bce) ordered the colonisation of Corinth and of Carthage. It was not all philanthropy, and among the motives for the re-foundation were the following:

- The colonists were Roman freedmen, urban plebs and Caesar's veterans. These were volatile groups and giving them land without having to take land from Italians was a neat solution.

- Caesar probably realised that Corinth would again flourish, and would thus revive the collapsed economy of Greece.

- Strategically, Corinth could be vital for Caesar's campaigns into Dacia and Parthia. As part of that he planned a canal across the isthmus which would facilitate not only business but the movement of troops.

Thus, in its re-foundation, Corinth was a Roman, Latin-speaking city. However, over the next two centuries, for various reasons, the population gradually became more Greek and the language, too, changed, as shall be seen below. The population, meanwhile, grew enormously.

---

3. A rare instance when inequality worked to women's advantage.
4. This is not so clear. I think Cicero means that the "temporary" inhabitants who had camped within the ruined city were a tough looking lot, a condition which he (kindly?) attributes to contemplation of the ruins. It is an early example of the effect of environment on us.

2.1   ECONOMIC AND SOCIAL LIFE OF ROMAN CORINTH

In his important book on Roman Corinth, Donald Engels, associate professor of history at the University of Arkansas, tried to estimate how big Roman Corinth really was, and how did the inhabitants of Corinth make their living. The argument over population is complex and hypothetical. By looking at the physical extent of Corinth and calculating from the average population density of comparable ancient cities, Engels established that the population of urban Corinth was about 80,000 people, and about 20,000 for rural Corinth (allowing for a wide margin of error). This number grew from the original Roman colonisation which numbered about 3,000 people.

What about the economy? Classically, archaeologists have spoken of agro-towns and consumer cities. Which was Corinth? First of all, no town over the size of 20,000 can be regarded as an agro-town. This is chiefly because the distances travelled to maintain farms and transport products would exceed the potential gain. A consumer city lives from rents. The reasons against thinking of Corinth as a consumer city are these:

• Rents were low in the classical era and there was widespread ownership of land. This means that a maximum of 10% to 20% of those supported by agriculture could have earned a living from rents. This is a small portion of the total population of most ancient cities.

• Further, because of the relatively small territories of most ancient cities, the number of landlords living in the cities would have been restricted, and certainly some landlords preferred to live in the countryside.

Engels developed the concept of the 'service city', a city which lived from the provision of services otherwise unavailable in the region. In the case of Corinth, these can be divided into two kinds, primary and secondary.

• Primary services were: religious, educational, cultural and judicial.

• Secondary services included food, temporary lodging, public baths and latrines.

Primary services attracted the visitor, the secondary services were only needed once a visitor arrived in Corinth. In the case of primary services, to take one example, there is ample evidence that Corinth provided a great variety of cultic options – Greek, Roman and Oriental. Likewise, the evidence for educational establishments and the presence of famous rhetoricians living and working in Corinth is clear.

2.2 WHO WERE THE CORINTHIANS?

This question needs to be sharpened by adding a second question – In what period? – because the ethnic and linguistic identity of the city changed over the two hundred years since its re-foundation by Julius Caesar. That change was substantially a change from Romans (Latin speaking) to Greeks (Greek speaking). The evidence for the change is chiefly epigraphic. The causes are easy to understand.

- Firstly, a Latin island in a Greek sea could not hope to survive for long.

- Secondly, all cities before the nineteenth century were unable to replace their own population by simple reproduction – chiefly because living close together brought a great deal of disease. Thus, in antiquity, city populations were maintained by immigration, usually over a short distance. In the case of Corinth, this naturally meant an influx of Greeks.

Living close together brought a great deal of disease.

Originally, only about 3,000 colonists came. These were:

- freedmen from Rome;

- the urban poor; and

- Caesar's veterans.

The natural advantage of the site meant that the city prospered and grew enormously over the next 200 years, and as has been seen, eventually the population was around 100,000 (taking in the city and its rural area). These colonists were producers rather than literati, and this gave a special flavour to the city and its life. Later (having a Latin name was perceived as a snob value) the *arrivistes* soon forgot their origins. There was great social mobility; one could arrive the descendent of a slave, and reach practically to the top. Without being quite like Las Vegas, Corinth was a get-rich-quick city. Eventually, of course, there were, as always, rich and poor.

 ## The Christians

There was greater mobility in Corinth than in any other city of the time. It is probable that Paul's preaching appealed to the urban working class and the poor because Christianity was a religion which had no ethnic conditions. Its founder had been poor, and its main preacher supported himself by manual labour. Problems of authority were not to be unexpected in such a setting.

2.3 RELIGIONS IN CORINTH

Schematically, the general religious atmosphere in Corinth contained pagan cults, the local deities and the Romans cults.

- In the pagan cults, Poseidon and Aphrodite were important – not a surprise in a port town.

- The local deities reflected the social mix of Corinth: Athena, goddess of craftsmen, and Asklepios, the healing divinity.

- The Roman cults encouraged civic passivity: initially the emperor cult, and then various abstractions such as Victoria, Concordia, the Genius of the Colony, and such like.

- Other Eastern religions included not only Egyptian mystery religions but also Judaism.

Poseidon

Aphrodite

Athena

Asklepios

In practice, people seemed to have easily combined the various options. The difficulty for Paul was that these religions were woven into the very texture of society, especially in the trade guilds.

By now, it should be clear just how prosperous Roman Corinth really was, with its population being quite a mixture, and having a high quality of life in both the material and spiritual spheres. Everything in the city would have been a token of the protection of the 'pagan' gods.

3.   THE CHRISTIAN CORINTHIANS

If 1 *Corinthians* 1 is taken at face value one arrives at a simplistic, even romantic, view of the membership of the Corinthian community. Paul states that not all the Christians were wise, not all were powerful, and not all were of noble birth – which means that some were wise, some powerful and some of noble birth, though not necessarily the same people. This is confirmed by the apparent contradiction in 1 *Corinthians* 4 when Paul states to the Corinthians that they are clever, strong and honoured, and in so doing Paul puts himself down as the refuse of the earth. The rhetorical function of these statements is important.

3.1   THE NAMES WE KNOW

Writing of the Corinthians whose names we know, Gerd Theissen, professor of New Testament at the University of Heidelberg, Germany, summarises as follows:

> We can now give a summary of what we know about those Corinthian Christians known to us by name. Apart from Chloe's people we have (at a maximum) sixteen names. However, it is not always certain that those names come from Corinth. Lucius (Rom 16:21) is frequently identified with Luke, Luke being a familiar form of Lucius. Similarly, it has been assumed that Sosipater (Rom 16:21) is the Sopater of Beroea mentioned in *Acts* 20:4. Sosthenes, who is mentioned alongside Paul in the prescription of the First Letter to Corinth, could only be regarded as a Corinthian if identified with Sosthenes the synagogue ruler in Acts 18:17, which is by no means certain.
>
> (Theissen, Gerd: *The Social Setting of Pauline Christianity*, pp.94-95)

The criteria used by Theissen to discern the social standing of these various people are the ownership of a house, the rendering of services to Paul, the ability to travel around the empire and the holding of public office. The details are in the footnotes,[5] but schematically laid out, the results are as follows:

Name	House	Travel	Support	Office
Acaichus				
Aquila	✓	✓	✓	
Erastus		✓		✓
Fortunatus				
Gaius	✓			
Jason				
Crispus	✓			✓
Lucius				
Priscilla	✓	✓	✓	
Phoebe		✓	✓	
Quartus				
Sosipater				
Sosthenes		✓		✓
Stephanas	✓	✓	✓	
Titus Justus			✓	
Tertius				
Chloe's People				

Theissen concludes: 'The great majority of Corinthians known to us by name probably enjoyed high social status.'[6] Was it the case that Paul named only the prominent people? One gets the impression that Paul's Corinthians were remarkably loose in their morals. Even in antiquity the city had a name for licentiousness, as can be seen in the following citation from Cicero:

> Maritime cities also suffer a certain corruption and degeneration of morals; for they receive a mixture of strange languages and customs, and import foreign ways as well as foreign merchandise, so that none of their ancestral institutions can possibly remain unchanged. Even their inhabitants do not cling to their dwelling places, but are constantly being tempted far from home by soaring hopes and dreams; and even when their bodies stay at home, their thoughts nevertheless fare abroad and go wandering. In fact, no other influence did more to bring about the final overthrow of Carthage and Corinth, though they had long been tottering, than this scattering and dispersion of their citizens, due to the fact that the lust for trafficking and sailing the seas had caused them to abandon agriculture and the pursuit of arms. [Cicero: *On the Republic* 2:7-9]
>
> (Murphy-O'Connor *St Paul's Corinth*, p.49)

5. The relevant people are listed by Theissen as follows:
   Acaichus: 1 Cor 16:17; companion of Stephanas.
   Aquila: Rom 16:3; Act 18:2, 18, 26; 1 Cor 16:19; house-congregation; small business establishment; travel; support of apostles.
   Erastus: Rom 16:23; financial official of the city; probably later chosen aide; and in consequence, made a public gift; travel.
   Fortunatus: 1 Cor 16:17; companion of Stephanas.
   Gaius: Rom 16:23; 1 Cor 1:14; his house served the entire church and Paul. Connections with Erastus?
   Jason: Rom 16:21
   Crispus: 1 Cor 1:14; Acts 18:8; synagogue ruler; manager of a 'house'; his conversion to Christianity influenced others.
   Lucius: Rom 16;21
   Priscilla: See Aquila
   Phoebe: Rom 16:1-2; services rendered to Paul and the Church; travel.
   Quartus: Rom 16:23.
   Sosipater: Rom 16:21
   Sosthenes: 1 Cor 1:1; Acts 18:17 (?); synagogue ruler; travel.
   Stephanas: 1 Cor 1:16; 16:15; manager of a house; services rendered to the church; travel.
   Titus Justus: Acts 18:7; lodging for Paul.
   Tertius:Rom 16:22; scribe.
   Chloe's people:1 Cor 1:11.
6. Theissen: *The Social Setting of Pauline Christianity* p.95.

Did Paul's ethical advice confirm or challenge the prevailing ethos of Corinth?

However, the image of 1,000 temple prostitutes is one that belonged to the Hellenistic period though, no doubt, something of that piety continued in the Roman port. It is difficult to gauge the prevailing standards of morality because ethical attitudes are not often reflected in buildings – apart from the general ethic of the public good and the duty of the rich to patronise the cities. There is a certain dependence, therefore, on the written word – what has come down to us in the writings about popular philosophy and in the various faiths (to which may be added the chance personal insight from some text or other). In order that such a huge task might have manageable proportions, this unit will look at the background to the ethics, and especially the ethics of marriage, in St Paul. Did Paul's ethical advice confirm or challenge the prevailing ethos? Would it even have been understood? There is a double background here – one in Jewish tradition and one in Greco-Roman tradition. Bearing in mind that Paul was dealing with a community which was both Hellenistic Jewish and also gentile, both cultures need to be looked at briefly.

3.2   THE JEWISH TRADITION

Fig. 5: *Philo of Alexandria*

The Septuagint placed adultery at the top of the list of sins against one's neighbour.

Philo condemned any expression of sexuality, even within marriage, that was not for the purpose of procreation.

In general, in the Hebrew Bible there is a robust and perfectly natural attitude to marriage and procreation. However, beginning in the later books of the Hebrew Bible, and continuing in the New Testament, there is a general decline in the way in which sexuality is valued, and an associated tendency towards exaggerating its sinfulness. Thus, Philo – interpreting the Septuagint's re-ordering of the Ten Commandments to place adultery at the top of the list of sins against one's neighbour, even before murder – takes this to mean that adultery was the most serious sin of all. Philo also condemned any expression of sexuality, even within marriage, that was not for the purpose of procreation. A similarly cool attitude may be found at Qumran, where the practice was confirmed by the paucity of young and female skeletons found in the cemetery. In some of his teachings, Jesus was also at least apparently anti-familial and anti-marital, in spite of a later accommodation in the Christian tradition to the conventional wisdom.[7]

---

7.   Texts such as the following make awkward reading even today:
     Mt 8:21: Another of his disciples said to him, "Lord, first let me go and bury my father." [22]But Jesus said to him, "Follow me, and let the dead bury their own dead."
     Mt 10:34: "Do not think that I have come to bring peace to the earth; I have not come to bring peace, but a sword. [35]For I have come to set a man against his father, and a daughter against her mother, and a daughter-in-law against her mother-in-law;
     Mt 10:36 'and one's foes will be members of one's own household. [37]Whoever loves father or mother more than me is not worthy of me; and whoever loves son or daughter more than me is not worthy of me.
     Mt 19:10: 'His disciples said to him, "If such is the case of a man with his wife, it is better not to marry." [11]'But he said to them, "Not everyone can accept this teaching, but only those to whom it is given. [12]For there are eunuchs who have been so from birth, and there are eunuchs who have been made eunuchs by others, and there are eunuchs who have made themselves eunuchs for the sake of the kingdom of heaven. Let anyone accept this who can."'

3.3 HELLENISTIC TRADITION

In terms of mainstream philosophy, Greco-Roman thought regarded the household as the basic building block of society. However, in common with most ancient cultures, unconditional fidelity was demanded of the wife alone. There was no prohibition with male infidelity – as long as it was not with another man's wife. This was true also of ancient Greeks and ancient Romans. The state intervened to encourage 'family values', as can be seen in Augustus' (63 bce-14 ce) *Lex Julia de Adulteriis* which declared adultery a penal offence, carrying the mandatory and severe punishment of banishment. In spite of this, divorce remained common, and infidelity, even from the wife, was practically taken for granted. Interestingly, for Paul, banquets were considered especially risky moments. In the specifically Greek sphere, toleration of extra-marital affairs was usual, especially between master and (female) slave. This tolerance was not extended to women. A selection of sources of popular philosophy which addressed marriage and sexuality will now be examined.

Unconditional fidelity was demanded of the wife alone.

Divorce remained common, and infidelity, even from the wife, was practically taken for granted.

Cynicism

Fig. 6: *Diogenes of Athens* (4c. bce)

Cynicism is a tradition which goes back to the fourth century bce. It represented a challenge to conventional society and may be said to be anti-marriage. The life-style of a cynic was that of the bohemian drop-out at its minimalist best. They aimed at indifference – the ethics ranged from utter shamelessness (to prove indifference), to severe austerity (likewise to prove indifference). Possible links with Christianity range from the style of the wandering preacher (as in the Galilean Jesus) to the use of the diatribe in the letters of St Paul. The libertinism of the Corinthians might have found philosophical backing in this stream of philosophy, as can be read in I *Corinthians* 6:12 'All things are lawful for me', but not all things are beneficial. 'All things are lawful for me', but I will not be dominated by anything.

indifference

This saying has Stoic echoes. Behind the statement lies a question: Where do I situate sexuality – with the morally-neutral issues of food, drink, feast-days and so forth? The threat of such libertinism is that it resembles Christian liberty.

Stoicism

Fig. 7: *Zeno of Elea*

Stoicism is another word which has suffered from English adaptation. A stoic did not aim at a passionless existence ('stoic' in the modern sense), but rather at not being ruled by the passions. Hence, sexual enjoyment was not excluded, but adultery and extra-marital affairs were ruled out.

> The man is free who lives as he wishes, who is proof against compulsion and hindrances and violence, whose impulses are untrammelled, who gets what he wills to get and avoids what he wills to avoid.
> [Epictetus, *Discourse* IV]

3.4   I CORINTHIANS 7:29

> [29]I mean, brothers and sisters, the appointed time has grown short; from now on, let even those who have wives be as though they had none, [30]and those who mourn as though they were not mourning, and those who rejoice as though they were not rejoicing, and those who buy as though they had no possessions, [31]and those who deal with the world as though they had no dealings with it. For the present form of this world is passing away. (1 Cor 7:29-31)

An awareness of this background may help in understanding Paul's reactions to the extreme libertinism and asceticism. In this context, Paul is perceived negatively, with a miserable view of sexuality/marriage. In his own context, he appears as one who was trying to keep various tensions in balance. Against the prevailing Greco-Roman culture, and consonant with Jewish tradition, he was absolutely against adultery. Against Roman and Jewish tradition, he was against divorce, with some interesting exceptions. He gave a direct answer to libertines who maintained that sexual intercourse was as necessary to the body as food and drink, and just a morally neutral. Paul replied that food and drink are linked to the present world and will disappear with it. But sexual conduct touches on our belonging to Christ, and so it must befit a Christian. Therefore Paul resisted the extreme asceticism of some Corinthians, who would say that marriage itself was wrong. On the contrary, he maintained the essential goodness of marriage, in line with good Hebrew tradition:

Paul was absolutely against adultery.

Paul was against divorce, with some interesting exceptions.

> [3]The husband should give to his wife her conjugal rights, and likewise the wife to her husband. [4]For the wife does not have authority over her own body, but the husband does; likewise the husband does not have authority over his own body, but the wife does.[8] (1 Cor 7:3)

Of course, in the light of his eschatology (a purely Christian theme) he favours celibacy, a theme comprehensible to the Stoic tradition, even though the reason for it would have been incomprehensible.

---

8.   A text often not read beyond v.4a!

3.5 HOUSES AND CHURCHES

As a last step in examining the church of Corinth and the Corinthians, the social setting of Pauline Christianity is put to one side, and attention must turn to its physical setting, that is, its housing. For the first three centuries or so, Christian communities did not have public buildings at their disposal. Instead, as is well known, use was made of the houses of families which had become Christian. Just four houses from the Roman period in Corinth have been excavated. The villa at Anaploga is the only one to be dated to the time of Paul. Houses had, so to speak, private and public rooms, as today. The public spaces were the *atrium*, or central court, and the *triclinium* or dining room. In this particular house the *triclinium* has a floor are of 41.25m². The *atrium* has a floor area, including the *impluvium*, of 30m². These are regarded as typical dimensions.[9]

Using a working average of 55m² for the *atrium* and 36m² for the *triclinium*, one can imagine that accommodating 50 people would be difficult. In practice, the church must have met most often in smaller sub-groups. Not only that, if the groups were between 30 and 40 on average, the host would still have to split the group between the *triclinium* and the *atrium* – and the guests in the *triclinium* would have reclined, further reducing the space available. It was not unusual, even if hardly polite, to serve different refreshment to different guests – as Pliny has shown us.[10] This may well explain the problem mentioned in 1 *Corinthians* 11:17-34. Such a mixture of good manners and practicality would have destroyed what the eucharist was supposed to be about. Bearing in mind that the rich were the hosts and the poor the guests, it is not hard to imagine the fragility of the relationships. Finally, the entire Christian community at Corinth would probably have gathered together in its entirety only rarely, for want of adequate accommodation.

For the first three centuries or so, Christian communities did not have public buildings at their disposal.

atrium
triclinium
impluvium

Fig. 8: *Roman triclinium*

4.　CONCLUSION

This tour of Corinth has covered the main features of the great Greco-Roman city, including the imposing civic and religious buildings, but also included the back-streets and finally people's homes and lives. After a brief glance at geography and history, a picture of the economic and ethical life of Corinth was put together, before a specific examination was made of the Christians of the Roman city. Their economic and social background was examined, as were their prevailing attitudes to marriage and the size of the Christian community.

Corinthian conflict and the ensuing correspondence did not arise out of nothing (Latin: *ex nihilo*). When one speaks of Paul's letters to the Corinthians one ought not to think of Paul writing to the city, but to think concretely of those small but probably quite typical groups which together made up the fractious Corinthian community.

EXERCISE 2:

a) *What was the history of Corinth? Write 10 lines.*

b) *What were the philosophies and the religions of Corinth? Write 5 lines.*

9.　The famous House of the Vettii at Pompeii had a atrium of 42m² and a triclinium of 25.2m². The Villa of Good Fortune at Olynthus (SE of Thessalonica) had a triclinium of 29m² and an atrium with its impluviums of 100m². Data and calculations taken from Murphy-O'Connor, St Paul's Corinth.

10.　Murphy-O'Connor: St Paul's Corinth, p.167.

SECTION TWO:

1 CORINTHIANS 1-4

Fig. 9: 1 *Corinthians* 2:11-3.5

I.   INTRODUCTION

In general, the Corinthian correspondence provides the most extensive account of Paul's teachings in a concrete setting, with special emphasis on the problems in the church there. Furthermore, his concerns about his authority and the collection for the Jerusalem church are highlighted in these letters.

1 *Corinthians* is a long letter (16 chapters) and contains some of the best-loved passages in Paul's writing. Within it is found the 'hymn to love' (ch.13), the great meditation on the cross (ch.1) and some profound teaching on the resurrection (ch.15), as well as the Lord's Supper (ch.11).

2.   BACKGROUND

2.1   AUTHORSHIP AND TEXT

Papyrus 46

There is no dispute among scholars about the Pauline authorship of 1 *Corinthians*. The earliest extant copy is Papyrus 46, dated around 200 ce, which contains parts of chapters 1, 9, 14, 15 and 16. It is conserved partly in Dublin and partly in Vienna. The letter is cited in the *First Letter of Clement from Rome* (1 Clem 37:5; 47:1-3; 49:5) and by Ignatius of Antioch (Eph 16:1;18:1;Rom 5:1).

> ⁵Let us take our body as an example. The head without the feet is nothing; likewise, the feet without the head are nothing. Even the smallest parts of our body are necessary and useful to the whole body, yet all the members work together and unite in mutual subjection, that the whole body may be saved. (1 Clem 37:5)

and:

> [1]Take up the epistle of the blessed Paul the apostle. [2]What did he first write to you in the 'beginning of the Gospel'?[115] [3]Truly he wrote to you in the Spirit about himself and Cephas and Apollos, because even then you had split into factions. (1 Clem 47:1-3)

and:

> [5]Love unites us with God; 'love covers a multitude of sins';[118] love endures all things, is patient in all things. There is nothing coarse, nothing arrogant in love. Love knows nothing of schisms, love leads no rebellions, love does everything in harmony. In love all the elect of God were made perfect; without love nothing is pleasing to God. (1 Clem 49:5)

and:

> [1]Do not be misled, my brothers: those who adulterously corrupt households 'will not inherit the kingdom of God.'[23] (Eph 16:1)

and:

> [1]My spirit is a humble sacrifice for the cross, which is a stumbling block to unbelievers, but salvation and eternal life to us. 'Where is the wise? Where is the debater?'[25] Where is the boasting of those who are thought to be intelligent? (Eph 18:1)

and:

> [1]From Syria all the way to Rome I am fighting with wild beasts, on land and sea, by night and day, chained amidst ten leopards (that is, a company of soldiers) who only get worse when they are well-treated. Yet because of their mistreatment I am becoming more of a disciple; nevertheless 'I am not thereby justified.'[72] (Rom 5:1)

2.2 CONTEXT AND AUDIENCE

After Paul's evangelisation, which was successful, 1 *Corinthians* seems to have been written from Ephesus (16:8), and the mention of the collection for the Jerusalem church (16:1) indicates that this letter precedes the *Letter to the Romans*. Traditional dating would suggest that the founding of the church took place in 49-51 ce, as part of Paul's second missionary journey. Paul remained about eighteen months in Corinth and left behind a flourishing fledgling community. Some time later, Paul wrote an initial letter to the Corinthian church from Ephesus (a document which is no longer extant) in order to deal with some specific ethical issue faced by the new believers. But the Corinthians didn't really understand Paul, and misapplied his teaching. The church then wrote to Paul for clarification, and Paul's reply was carried by the messengers mentioned in 1 *Corinthians* 16:15-17. This is the letter now known as 1 *Corinthians*. At the time of writing, Paul intended to visit Corinth.

Paul had received a report describing various problems at Corinth which had arisen in his absence. These concerned sexual morality, the eucharist, the charismatic gifts and the resurrection. Before going into all these issues in detail, Paul tackled the problem posed by the new leadership in the community, one which apparently was undermining his position as the 'father'. The new leaders were excellent speakers and put a great deal of emphasis on 'wisdom'. The various points can be summarised as follows:

• The Corinthians viewed Jesus mainly as 'the Lord of glory' (2:8) and took little or no account of his crucifixion as an event of saving significance.

• They understood themselves, as believers, to be the recipients of special religious wisdom and privileged with special knowledge about God (4:10; 8:2), and perhaps regarded this as a sign of their own present reigning with Christ in glorious triumph.

• They valued spiritual gifts highly, and those who could display extraordinary ones – particularly the gift of ecstatic utterance (speaking in tongues) – advanced their religious standing within the congregation (chapters 12-14).

• At least some in the congregation, perhaps because they believed themselves to be sharing already in Christ's glorious reign, had all but ceased to hope for anything beyond this life (15:12-19).

• Finally, some, or perhaps even most, of the congregation believed that in reigning with Christ they were delivered from the need to worry about questions of right and wrong or about distinguishing between moral and immoral actions. To characterise this view, Paul cited, or perhaps himself devised, the slogan, 'Everything is permissible for me' (6:12; 10:23). Others, however, seem to have embraced the almost opposite view, convinced that in reigning with Christ they were required to distance themselves as far as possible from the moral stain of worldly involvements (for example, sexual relations) as indicated by a statement that Paul quoted from a letter the church had written to him (7:1b).

In summary, there seems to have been a four-fold problematic:

a) christologically: the Corinthians took little or no account of Jesus' death (1-4);

b) soteriologically: they misconstrued the meaning of freedom in Christ (5-7);

c) ecclesiologically: they neglected the corporate dimension of life in Christ (8-14); and

d) eschatologically: they failed to appreciate the apostle's dialectical understanding of salvation as both 'already' and 'not yet' (15).

3. FOREGROUND

3.1 CONTENTS

The contents of 1 *Corinthians* may be outlined as follows:

1:10-4:21	divisions in the community
5-7	moral issues in tension with society
8-11	community meals: food sacrificed to idols / the eucharist
12-14	the charismatic gifts
15	the resurrection

3.2 A LETTER AND A SPEECH

Clearly, at the beginning and at the end, one finds the classic beginning and ending of a letter, with the usual extended thanksgiving.

1:1-3	Opening greetings
1:4-9	Thanksgiving
16:1-16	Detailed final instructions
16:17-21	Closing greetings.

Verses	Letter	Rhetoric	Topic
1:1-3	Superscript		Greetings
1:4-9	Thanksgiving	Introduction	Key terms are introduced
1:10-17	Letter body	Statement of Facts	Factions and divisions in Corinth
1:18-4:21		Proof 1	The Corinthians attachment to fine speech
5:1-11:1		Proof 2	Specific issues: sexual immorality, litigation, marriage, food sacrificed to idols, freedom
11:2-14:40		Proof 3	Worship: hair style, disorder the the Lord's Supper, charismatic gifts and prophecy
15		Proof 4	The resurrection of believers
16		Postscript	Forthcoming visits, summary

EXERCISE 3:

a) *What were the problems facing Paul in writing 1 Corinthians? Write 5 lines.*

b) *What do we know about the authorship of 1 Corinthians? Write 5 lines.*

4. COMMENTARY

Chapters 1-4 will now be examined in detail. These chapters can be read using the categories of rhetoric as follows:

Introduction	1:4-9
Statement of Facts	1:10-17
Thesis in three parts	1:17
Proof 1: wisdom / foolishness	1:18-2:5
Proof 2: Spirit wisdom	2:6-16
Proof 3: The apostles	3:1-17
Refutation 1: Wisdom / foolishness	3:18-23
Refutation 2: The apostles (a)	4:1-7
Refutation 3: The apostles (b)	4:8-13
Conclusion	4:14-21

4.1 INTRODUCTION (1:4-9)

⁴I give thanks to my God always for you because of the grace of God that has been given you in Christ Jesus, ⁵for in every way you have been enriched in him, in speech and knowledge of every kind – ⁶just as the testimony of Christ has been strengthened among you – ⁷so that you are not lacking in any spiritual gift as you wait for the revealing of our Lord Jesus Christ. ⁸He will also strengthen you to the end, so that you may be blameless on the day of our Lord Jesus Christ. ⁹God is faithful; by him you were called into the fellowship of his Son, Jesus Christ our Lord. (1 Cor 1:4-9)

The thanksgiving, or introduction, alludes to the many problems facing the Corinthian church: speech, spiritual gifts, blameless fellowship, etc. This praise is not cynical. While there are problems, and Paul will name them, at the same time, he thinks their basic gifts are good and worthy of praise. It is an instance of the Pauline tendency to praise first and then encourage / admonish.

4.2 STATEMENT OF FACTS (1:10-17)

¹⁰Now I appeal to you, brothers and sisters, by the name of our Lord Jesus Christ, that all of you be in agreement and that there be no divisions among you, but that you be united in the same mind and the same purpose. ¹¹For it has been reported to me by Chloe's people that there are quarrels among you, my brothers and sisters. ¹²What I mean is that each of you says, 'I belong to Paul,' or 'I belong to Apollos,' or 'I belong to Cephas,' or 'I belong to Christ.' ¹³Has Christ been divided? Was Paul crucified for you? Or were you baptised in the name of Paul? ¹⁴I thank God that I baptised none of you except Crispus and Gaius, ¹⁵so that no one can say that you were baptised in my name. ¹⁶(I did baptise also the household of Stephanas; beyond that, I do not know whether I baptised anyone else.) ¹⁷For Christ did not send me to baptise but to proclaim the gospel, and not with eloquent wisdom, so that the cross of Christ might not be emptied of its power. (1 Cor 1:10-17)

The factionalism in Corinth seems to be very strong.

Factions can be expected when communities are house-based, but the factionalism in Corinth seems to have been very strong. The rhetorical questions Paul used were very powerful in undermining these attachments to parties and personalities.

4.3   THE THESIS IN THREE PARTS (1:17)

> [17]For Christ did not send me to baptise but to proclaim the gospel, and not with eloquent wisdom, so that the cross of Christ might not be emptied of its power.

It is always possible to divide a thesis into a number of subsections. The technical term for this is a *partitio*, and Paul seems to have used this here. The three parts of verse 17 correspond to the three proofs and three refutations which follow.

partitio

Thesis	Proof	Refutation
[17]For Christ did not send me to baptise but to proclaim the gospel,	Proof 3: I planted but Apollos watered	Refutation 2: the relative importance of the apostles
and not with eloquent wisdom,	Proof 2: there is a spiritual wisdom	Refutation 1: the wisdom of this world is foolishness
so that the cross of Christ might not be emptied of its power.	Proof 1: the message of the cross	Refutation 3: the foolishness of the apostles

Paul's overall aim in 1-4 is to shatter the Corinthians attachment to party and personality, especially any attachment based on merely human eloquence.

4.4   PROOF 1   (1:18-2:5)

In the first proof, Paul starts out with the strongest possible approach, that is, the cross of Jesus. This is so paradoxical an event that any over-attachment to reason or wisdom is undermined. It is a very powerful opening gambit. Paul follows it by asking the Corinthians to register the place of paradox in the Christian proclamation by looking at themselves. Because of their mostly humble beginnings, they themselves were an example of how God chooses what is weak and humble. The vulnerability of the Corinthians on this score meant that they were really listening to Paul. However, attention might come at the cost of goodwill: after all, Who likes to told that they are weak and foolish?

paradox

With a very deft move, Paul takes the harm out of this by going on to use himself as an example of weakness and foolishness. This had a double purpose. It served to put Paul at the same level as the Corinthians, and took the harm out of his previous 'insult'. At the same time, it acknowledged the Corinthian critique of Paul and used it to his advantage. Impressed as they are by the fluency and eloquence of Apollos, Paul claimed that any lack of these gifts was more in tune with the cross. It was also vital for Paul that their faith did not depend on his eloquence, or indeed anyone else's.

4.5   PROOF 2   (2:6-16)

Paul does not deny that the desire for wisdom is good. But there are different kinds of wisdom. Some wisdom is merely human – the kind of thinking purveyed by the popular philosophers of the day. And some wisdom is truly from God. This wisdom bears the authentic mark of transcendence: 'What no eye has seen, nor ear heard, nor the human heart conceived, what God has prepared for those who love him' (1 Cor 2:9). This wisdom is not the fruit of human eloquence or human achievement; it is a gift. This wisdom can be acquired, but never in such a way that it can be used to set one person above another. This wisdom is from God and requires its own language of guarded eloquence.

Now we have received not the spirit of the world, but the Spirit that is from God, so that we may understand the gifts bestowed on us by God. And we speak of these things in words not taught by human wisdom but taught by the Spirit, interpreting spiritual things to those who are spiritual. (1 Cor 2:12-13)

4.6 PROOF 3 (3:1-17)

Paul freely admits at the start that he had left Corinth before complete evangelisation had occurred. Thus it was that he baptised hardly anyone and that Apollos completed his work. In order to establish the relative significance of the apostles, Paul used a very careful image:

> ⁵What then is Apollos? What is Paul? Servants through whom you came to believe, as the Lord assigned to each. ⁶I planted, Apollos watered, but God gave the growth. (1 Cor 3:5)

Verse 6 leads to a natural climax: God gave the growth, while leaving in place the chronological priority of Paul, 'I planted'. Even with the field metaphor, Paul leaves open the question of future assessment and judgment. To explore the idea of assessment further, Paul changed the metaphor from 'field' to 'building'. This allowed him to speak of foundations, and of course there can be only one foundation, Christ.

4.7 REFUTATION I (3:18-23)

Fig. 10: *Peter and Paul*

In clinching his arguments on the relative importance of those who brought the gospel to Corinth, Paul warned the Corinthians about having any false attachment to merely human wisdom. The true wisdom from God is paradoxical, requiring us to be foolish. In a reversal of everyday perspective, any human attachment to this or that leader is absolutely beside the point. There is a much wider perspective:

So let no one boast about human leaders. For all things are yours, whether Paul or Apollos or Cephas or the world or life or death or the present or the future – all belong to you, and you belong to Christ, and Christ belongs to God. (1 Cor 3:21-23)

4.8   REFUTATION 2   (4:1-7)

Divine assessment is the only valid one, and Paul proclaims himself indifferent to human assessment. This is both true and not true at the same time.

- It is true because Paul, like the Corinthians, looks forward to true assessment by God and not by others.

- It is not true because what they think of him matters to Paul.

Paul would claim that his concern arises not from self-preoccupation but from a desire to draw them back to the authentic experience of the gospel.

4.9   REFUTATION 3   (4:8-13)

Paul then returns to his own experience. In a passage loaded with irony and decorated with literary techniques he showed that he can be quite rhetorical, while simultaneously denying its importance.

4.10 CONCLUSION   (4:14-21)

This temporary conclusion shows all the marks of a *peroratio*. It summarises the contents by noting the problems which have arisen (spiritual arrogance) and his own role in their lives ('you do not have many fathers').

> ⁴I am not writing this to make you ashamed, but to admonish you as my beloved children. ¹⁵For though you might have ten thousand guardians in Christ, you do not have many fathers. Indeed, in Christ Jesus I became your father through the gospel. ¹⁶I appeal to you, then, be imitators of me. ¹⁷For this reason I sent you Timothy, who is my beloved and faithful child in the Lord, to remind you of my ways in Christ Jesus, as I teach them everywhere in every church. ¹⁸But some of you, thinking that I am not coming to you, have become arrogant. ¹⁹But I will come to you soon, if the Lord wills, and I will find out not the talk of these arrogant people but their power. ²⁰For the kingdom of God depends not on talk but on power. ²¹What would you prefer? Am I to come to you with a stick, or with love in a spirit of gentleness? (1 Cor 4:14-21)

5.   CONCLUSION

At the start of the letter, Paul tackled the general problems in the Corinthian church before addressing the more specific issues. The starting point of the cross will remain important throughout the letter.

EXERCISE 4:

a) *What was Paul's understanding of the cross in 1 Corinthians 1-4? Write 5 lines.*

b) *In 1 Corinthians 1-4, how did Paul understand his mission in relation to others? Write 5 lines.*

SECTION THREE:

THE LORD'S SUPPER

(1 Cor 11:17-34)

I. INTRODUCTION

1 *Corinthians* 11:17-34 is the earliest existing account of the Lord's Supper and so it is of very special interest – not only in terms of wording but also in terms of practice. It finds its place in the wider setting of issues in the community which Paul has to face.

It may seem puzzling that Paul did not mention the Lord's Supper more frequently. Had there been some mention of it in *Romans* (that overview of Christian teaching and practice) it would not have seemed out of place. However, it was precisely because the Corinthian celebration of the eucharist was particularly divided that Paul discussed it quite penetratingly in chapter 11.

2. STRUCTURE

Gordon Fee (Professor Emeritus of New Testament Studies, Regent College, Vancouver) gives the following structure for the issues arising in 1 *Corinthians*.

I. *Introduction* (1:1-9)
    A. Salutation (1:1-3)
    B. Thanksgiving (1:4-9)

II. In *Response to Reports* (1:10-6:20)
    A. A divided church (1:10-4:20)
    B. Immorality and litigation (5:1-6:20)

III. In *Response to the Corinthian Letter*
    A. Marriage and related matters (7:1-40)
    B. Food sacrificed to idols (8:1-11:1)
    C. Women and men in worship (11:2-16)
    D. Abuse of the Lord's Supper (11:17-34)
    E. Spiritual gifts (12-14)
    F. The Resurrection (15)
    G. The Collection (16:1-11)
    H. About the coming of Apollos (16:12)

IV. *Concluding Matters*
    A. Concluding Exhortations (16:13-18)
    B. Final Greetings (16:19-24)

3.   THE LORD'S SUPPER

As has been seen from archaeology, Christians in Corinth could really meet only in larger houses which enjoyed an *atrium* and a *triclinium*, that is, in the residence of a wealthy member. This severely limited the possible numbers, and probably made the poor feel uncomfortable. Furthermore, it was usual to make distinctions between the guests, as can be seen from the following quote:

> I happened to be dining with a man, though no particular friend of his, whose elegant economy, as he called it, seemed to me a sort of stingy extravagance. The best dishes were set in front of himself and a select few, and the cheap scraps of food before the rest of the company. He had even put the wine into tiny little flasks, divided into three categories, not with the idea of giving his guests the opportunity of choose, but to make it impossible for them to refuse what they were given. One lot was intended for himself and for us, another for his lesser friends (all his friends are graded), and the third for his and our freedmen.
>
> ('Letters, 2:6', in Murphy-O'Connor, J.: *St Paul's Corinth*, p.167)

3.1   THE SUPPER OF THE LORD

Any discussion of this passage needs to be set in the context of Paul's overall reflections on the eucharist. First of all, the topic comes up formally only in 1 *Corinthians* 11, which raises some questions about its centrality in Paul's Christianity. This is partly the result of Paul's theologising by context; but it places inevitable limits on what can be said about the eucharist in his view. In terms of background, the theory of 'mystery religions' as the origin of the eucharist is discounted nowadays. The parallels have been exaggerated. The overall context of Jesus' ministry – the Passover and the eating of the sacrifices of the Temple – provide sufficient background to grasp what was going on.

The question of the historical origin of the sacrament is a tricky one which calls for careful handling. A study by John P. Meier (professor of New Testament at the University of Notre Dame, Indiana) offers a reasonable account of the issues involved. In brief, there are two versions of the origin of the sacrament of the eucharist, one in *Mark* and *Matthew*, and the other in *Paul* and *Luke*. Both probably come from a common source, going back ultimately to a single final meal which Jesus held and in which he said significant words and did significant actions with the bread and wine. Both sources probably go back to an original ,and both show signs of liturgical development. The general lack of balance in the phrases in *Paul* and *Luke* would suggest that this is perhaps the more original version, with additions.

Mt 26:26-28	Mk 14:22-24	Luke 22:19-20	I Cor 11:23-25
[26]While they were eating, Jesus took a loaf of bread, and after blessing it he broke it, gave it to the disciples, and said, 'Take, eat; this is my body.' [27]Then he took a cup, and after giving thanks he gave it to them, saying, 'Drink from it, all of you; [28]for this is my blood of the covenant, which is poured out for many for the forgiveness of sins.	[22]While they were eating, he took a loaf of bread, and after blessing it he broke it, gave it to them, and said, 'Take; this is my body.' [23]Then he took a cup, and after giving thanks he gave it to them, and all of them drank from it. [24]He said to them, 'This is my blood of the covenant, which is poured out for many.'	[19]Then he took a loaf of bread, and when he had given thanks, he broke it and gave it to them, saying, 'This is my body, which is given for you. Do this in remembrance of me.' [20]And he did the same with the cup after supper, saying, 'This cup that is poured out for you is the new covenant in my blood.'	[23]The Lord Jesus on the night when he was betrayed took a loaf of bread, [24]and when he had given thanks, he broke it and said, 'This is my body that is for you. Do this in remembrance of me.' [25]In the same way he took the cup also, after supper, saying, 'This cup is the new covenant in my blood. Do this, as often as you drink it, in remembrance of me.'

According to Meier, the earlier version resembled something like this:

> he took bread, and giving thanks [or: pronouncing a blessing], broke [it] and said: 'This is my body.' Likewise also the cup, after supper, saying: 'This cup is the covenant in my blood.
>
> (Meier, J.P.: 'The Eucharist at the Last Supper – Did it Happen?' in *Theology Digest*, 42 (1995) 335-352)

Presumably, the words of Jesus are older than the narrative surrounding them. The notable Pauline additions are the liturgical instructions and the addition of 1 *Corinthians* 11:25b-26.

> [24]and when he had given thanks, he broke it and said, 'This is my body that is for you. Do this in remembrance of me.' [25]In the same way he took the cup also, after supper, saying, 'This cup is the new covenant in my blood. Do this, as often as you drink it, in remembrance of me.' [26]For as often as you eat this bread and drink the cup, you proclaim the Lord's death until he comes. (1 Cor 11:24)

Writing to the Corinthians around 55 ce, Paul reminded them of what he told them around 51 ce, by recalling what he himself received around the time of his conversion, in 35 ce or thereabouts. The links are old and reliable. Paul's own reflections are influenced, of course, by his own theology of Christ's sacrificial death and of participation in Christ.

The questions which arise are not only theological, but ethical, that is, they are concerned with community customs. The Lord's Supper was still fully embedded in a meal and had not yet become a separate celebration. According to the practice of the time, each guest brought and ate his or her own food, or else it was put on a common table. Some came early and ate before the others. Those arriving late would find less to eat, or the best food gone. There would also have been no space in the *triclinium* for late-comers who might be dishonoured by having to sit in the *atrium*.

Furthermore, the traditional dinner-party often took place in two stages. A first table would be served followed by a break. Then the guests would have a symposium, to which other guests might be invited for light desert and drinks. It may be that the rich people who hosted the meal may have been treating the eucharist as the 'symposium part' of the meal only. That would mean some people were invited only to the 'afters' which, in practice, excluded some people from the other, substantial meal. That is possible. Against it is the idea that Paul speaks of only one meal. It may be that the breaking of the bread began the meal and the cup closed it, in which case, by not waiting for the others, they literally excluded them from the supper.

EXERCISE 5:

a) *What was the social setting for the Lord's Supper in Corinth? Write 5 lines.*

b) *Which are the two traditions of the Lord's Supper in the New Testament? Write 5 lines.*

4.   LITURGICAL PRACTICE

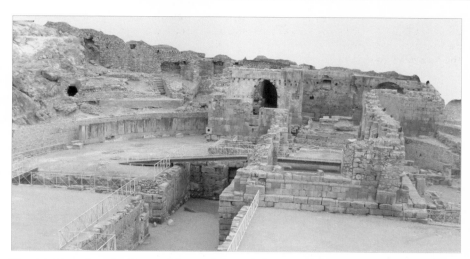

Fig. 11: *Remains of a Roman House of the period*

4.1   THE ABUSE OF FEEDING ONESELF

1 *Corinthians* 11:17-22

> [17]Now in the following instructions I do not commend you, because when you come together it is not for the better but for the worse. [18]For, to begin with, when you come together as a church, I hear that there are divisions among you; and to some extent I believe it. [19]Indeed, there have to be factions among you, for only so will it become clear who among you are genuine. [20]When you come together, it is not really to eat the Lord's supper. [21]For when the time comes to eat, each of you goes ahead with your own supper, and one goes hungry and another becomes drunk. [22]What! Do you not have homes to eat and drink in? Or do you show contempt for the church of God and humiliate those who have nothing? What should I say to you? Should I commend you? In this matter I do not commend you! (1 Cor 11:17-22)

Commendations at the beginning and the end frame this passage. This was an honour/shame society and to find the founding father so publicly 'not commending' would have been a source not only of unease but more importantly of shame. The reason for the non-commendation was their manner of 'coming together'. Coming together is a key term here – which recurs no fewer than five times. As the term is also found in 1 *Corinthians* 14:23 and 26 it has a technical feel to it, meaning the official gathering of the community.

Corinth was an honour/shame society.

> [23]If, therefore, the whole church comes together and all speak in tongues, and outsiders or unbelievers enter, will they not say that you are out of your mind? (1 Cor 14:23)

And,

> 26What should be done then, my friends? When you come together, each one has a hymn, a lesson, a revelation, a tongue, or an interpretation. Let all things be done for building up. (1 Cor 14:26)

Verse 18 recalls the divisions already discussed in 1:10-12 where people were taking sides on the basis of who spoke well. There was deep division in the church as such. Verse 19 seems very ironic and forceful. The rhetorical effect is to trigger a desire to be in the 'tried and tested' group. This begins the extension of the analysis of divisions, in that Paul wanted to suggest that these divisions were of more than sociological interest.

Verse 20 continues verse 18 and sets out a blunt thesis: they seemed to be celebrating the Lord's Supper, but were not. This is the only time in the New Testament that the eucharist is called the Lord's Supper and therefore it is not clear as to whether the language is traditional or Pauline. The noun is traditional, but what of the adjective? The literal translation would be 'lordish', and the meaning is something like 'belonging to the Lord', 'consecrated to the Lord' or 'in honour of the Lord'. The adjective contrasts sharply with 'one's own' in verse 21.

They seemed to be celebrating the Lord's Supper, but were not.

Verse 21 has given rise to considerable discussion. Was the problem being addressed one of intense individualism? Was it a question of some people eating beforehand, that is, apart from, the rest? This would mean that the rich were feasting ahead. Could it simply be a lack of sharing with the poor? Thus, although they came together as a church, each one was treated 'privately'. The evidence from Pliny plays a part here. Anyone humiliating those less fortunate would have been a source of anxiety in the Roman empire. However, within the Christian assembly it should not occur at all, and so Paul's words in verse 22 are especially challenging.

4.2   THE TRADITION

1 *Corinthians* 11:23-26

> 23For I received from the Lord what I also handed on to you, that the Lord Jesus on the night when he was betrayed took a loaf of bread, 24and when he had given thanks, he broke it and said, 'This is my body that is for you. Do this in remembrance of me.' 25In the same way he took the cup also, after supper, saying, 'This cup is the new covenant in my blood. Do this, as often as you drink it, in remembrance of me.' 26For as often as you eat this bread and drink the cup, you proclaim the Lord's death until he comes. (1 Cor 11:23-26)

This small unit is set apart by the use of 'Lord' and 'bread' at both the beginning and the end.

This is part of the pre-Pauline tradition to which Paul occasionally turns. This is an exceptional moment where Paul cites directly a saying which will re-appear in the synoptic gospels. Lots of questions can be asked: Was it the wording, the meaning or the text which provided an answer to the problem in the Corinthian church?

Although the four accounts of the Lord's Supper which have come down to us resemble each other, there are differences:

- Luke and Paul have 'give thanks' instead of 'bless';

- Luke and Paul have no blessing over the cup;

- Luke and Paul do not mention that all present drank from the cup; and

- Luke and Paul have a different saying over the cup.

The remembrance theme is strong in Paul. This might be a function of his argument (the Corinthians had forgotten the purpose of the meal) rather than a matter of tradition.

Paul's argument is based on received Christian tradition. Jewish technical terms (which come up again in 15:1-3) are 'used', 'received' and 'passed on'. What does he mean by 'from the Lord'? Probably not a direct revelation (in spite of Galatians 1:11-12 and 15-17). Probably it means 'as if from the Lord'. The important thing is that the meaning of the meal comes from the Lord. It is important that he uses 'Lord', that is, the risen Lord present in the community.

The meaning of the meal comes from the Lord.

This action with the bread and wine belongs within the range of prophetic gestures which encapsulate a message or a role or a word from God.

a) The word 'body' is semitic imagery, meaning the 'whole self'. Later on, important questions about the mode of the presence of Christ in the eucharist cannot be answered on the basis of this text because they have not been asked.

b) The giving of the body probably pointed historically to the cross – when Jesus gave himself – symbolised by the bread and wine.

c) The addition of 'for you' is unique to Paul and Luke and is more probably a reference to Isaiah 53:12. Thus, for Jesus himself, this is almost certainly a prophetic symbolic action, by which he anticipated his death and interpreted it in the light of scripture.

For Jesus himself, this is almost certainly a prophetic symbolic action, by which he anticipated his death and interpreted it in the light of scripture.

The words about the cup specify things further. The blood is a reference to life, (thus Gen 9:4; Lev 17:11, 14; Dt 12:23, etc.; see Jn 6:53-54) and in this context it summons the idea of a life that is given for others. The covenant resonance also evokes the Passover.

As regards the word 'remembrance', there is a large body of literature on it. The issues raised concern the following:

a) it deals with some complex usage of the word in the Old Testament and other Jewish literature;

b) it questions Jesus' own intent in the light of this usage; and

c) it involves Paul's own understanding.

In the Old Testament, the idea of memorial (Hebrew: *zikkron*) had a strong meaning which suggested participation in a past event. Jesus' reading was like that: any future remembrance will be as though the community had actually

This touches on the community's remembering, which allows the past to be powerfully and effectively present, defining, forming and nourishing its life.

been there. Paul's point here is that the Corinthians are mistaken, precisely because they forget in whose remembrance all this was being celebrated. This touches on the community's remembering, which allows the past to be powerfully and effectively present, defining, forming and nourishing its life.

Verse 26 is especially important:

> [26]For as often as you eat this bread and drink the cup, you proclaim the Lord's death until he comes. (1 Cor 11:26)

a)   'For' introduces an explanation;

b)   the word-order puts the emphasis on this death, the cost of self-giving;

c)   Paul picks up the precise language of the final repetition;

d)   this in turn picks up the eating of the bread, so as to include both parts of the meal in the explanation and the emphasis on the fact that both the bread and the cup proclaim Christ's death; and

e)   the expression 'until' might not have only durative force, but purpose; that is, it is suggesting 'in order that he may come'.

proclamation of the supper
practice of the participants

But the Corinthians do not proclaim the death of the Lord, which was the free gift of love for others. The contrast between the proclamation of the supper and the practice of the participants is amplified in the next section.

B'   Discerning the Body

> [27]Whoever, therefore, eats the bread or drinks the cup of the Lord in an unworthy manner will be answerable for the body and blood of the Lord. [28]Examine yourselves, and only then eat of the bread and drink of the cup. [29]For all who eat and drink without discerning the body, eat and drink judgement against themselves. [30]For this reason many of you are weak and ill, and some have died. [31]But if we judged ourselves, we would not be judged. [32]But when we are judged by the Lord, we are disciplined so that we may not be condemned along with the world. (1 Cor 11:27-32)

Paul begins to draw together his conclusions for the Corinthians. 'Unworthy' has two potential meanings:

a)   not being worthy, not meriting, and in that sense unworthily; and

b)   improperly, in the sense of not corresponding to what should happen.

The meaning here is not so much personal, spiritual worthiness, but impropriety, improperly participating in the eucharist.

Verse 29 provides a key:

> [29]For all who eat and drink without discerning the body, eat and drink judgment against themselves. (1 Cor 11:29)

It is not possible to receive Christ 'spiritually' while rejecting him in others, because Christ is one.

In a celebration where the 'community dimension' is absent, Paul would say that the Lord's Supper is not taking place.

The body in question is the social body of the Corinthian church. In dishonouring and excluding some of its members, the community failed to discern that this was the body of Christ. Discerning the body of Christ means accepting into one's life the whole body of Christ: it is not possible to receive Christ 'spiritually' while rejecting him in others, because Christ is one. In a celebration where the 'community dimension' is reduced or even absent, Paul would say that the Lord's Supper is not taking place. There is potential here for a thorough critique of the common experience of the eucharist.

The language Paul uses is very strong, suggesting liability. Paul's concern was not with the sacred elements, but with the action. To miss the point of the proclamation, is to miss the point of his death and to align oneself with those who caused his death in the first place. This sets in motion the whole chain of forensic

UNIT FIVE
SECTION THREE

language which follows. A judgement theme runs throughout the passage which must not be forgotten. The unsettling verse 30 is probably not a general spiritual principle, but an *ad hoc* application to what is going on in Corinth.

A'   *Mutual Hospitality*

[33]So then, my brothers and sisters, when you come together to eat, wait for one another. [34]If you are hungry, eat at home, so that when you come together, it will not be for your condemnation. About the other things I will give instructions when I come. (1 Cor 11:33-34)

The advice in the end is immensely practical: wait for one another. As usual, Paul has given his theological understanding, and then draws a conclusion. If you are that hungry, then have something to eat at home before the community comes together.

5.   CONCLUSIONS FOR TODAY

The Lord's Supper is a sacrament, a symbolic meal. The words and the actions over the bread and wine enable a double disclosure to take place.

- The first disclosure is that of the Lord himself. As a memorial meal, the participants are present, through the sacrament, at the first Lord's Supper. Once again, the Lord gives himself to all, so that they might come to him in faith.

As a memorial meal, the participants were present, through the sacrament, at the first Lord's Supper.

- The second disclosure is the mutual belonging of all participants in the one body of Christ.

These two disclosures cannot be separated – because Christ is one. It is not possible to say 'yes' to him in one disclosure and 'no' to him in another. This is the discernment of the body that Paul has in mind. 'For just as the body is one and has many members, and all the members of the body, though many, are one body, so it is with Christ' (1 Cor 12:12-13).

The common experience of the eucharist today could easily fall under the same critique. It is not that we do not wait for each other, but that the disclosure of mutual belonging and mutual acceptance is practically absent. Participants are present more as individuals than as members of a community. The problem here is not so much the liturgy but the lack of any real sense of a community of faith, before and after the liturgy.

Participants were present more as individuals that as a community.

EXERCISE 6:

a) *What is meant by the 'discerning the body' in I Corinthians I I? Write 5 lines.*

b) *What are the practical consequences of a renewed theology for today's celebration of the eucharist? Write 5 lines.*

SECTION FOUR:
THE HYMN TO LOVE

(1 Cor 13)

I. INTRODUCTION

An examination of 1 *Corinthians* 13 (one of the most loved passage in the Bible) will show that Paul was not just writing poetry. As always, there is a relationship between his text and what was going on in the community in Corinth. The Corinthians seem to have been suffering from two problems.

- The first was an exaggerated attachment to spiritual gifts, especially the more 'flashy' ones. The charismatic gifts as such were very important to Paul and to the Corinthians. As was seen in relation to *Galatians*, Paul was quite ready to call to mind such experiences whenever the need arose. But the problem here was a kind of competitiveness, a spiritual contest, which is surely a distortion of what the gifts were meant to be.

- A second issue – one to do with the use of the spiritual gifts – was the disordered nature of their worship. In particular, Paul was concerned that if some interested outsider came to take part in the eucharist, such a person might be bewildered rather than uplifted. Paul, therefore, faced a number of challenges in the community, and his reply is found in the context of chapters 12 to 14.

1.2 I CORINTHIANS 12-14

a) *Concentric Patterns*

palindrome

The palindrome (words or verses reading alike forwards or backwards) helps to illustrate the structure of the chapters. An example of a palindrome would be the first words supposedly spoken by Adam to Eve, 'Madam I'm Adam'. As you can see, the letters read the same backwards and forwards. There are plenty of these: a simple one is 'a man, a plan, a canal – Panama!'. And there is a famous one about Napoleon: 'Able was I e're I saw Elba'.

UNIT FIVE
SECTION FOUR

That sort of structure was known to the ancients and was used frequently in the literature of the Bible. For instance: 'I am who I am', which gives the pattern, ABA^1. And in Jesus' teaching there is: 'The first shall be last and last shall be first'; and 'the one who exalts himself shall be humbled and the one who humbles himself shall be exalted'. The pattern in both cases is ABB^{1}A^1. Now this sort of patterning was commonly used, not only for word-games or even for short sentences, but also for larger bodies of material.

In 2 *Corinthians* 12-14, there is a large pattern ABA^1, and it is quite simply laid out:

A	B	A^1
12	13	14
diversity	love	order

Usually (not always) the key will be in the centre, with the problem and solution on either side. Paul takes two steps: first he wants to show that diversity is good, then he wants to show that love is the most important gift of the spirit, and therefore for the building up of the Church it is more important than personal experience. The important conclusion he draws in A^1 is that prophecy is to be preferred to speaking in tongues. The sequence is important. He sees diversity and thinks that it is good; he then thinks that things can be put in some order of importance, and the supreme position must be given to love. The criterion of building up the Church becomes the criterion for finding the relationship between prophecy and tongues and their relative importance. In this way Paul does not deny the validity of their experience: gifts are good, diversity is good. But a sharper insight permits a careful balancing between the two. Paul's stages are reasonable clear:

Prophecy is to be preferred to speaking in tongues.

- first he affirms diversity (1);

- then he praises love (2); and

- then he places prophecy above tongues (3), precisely because it builds up and is, therefore, loving.

In this way the layout provides a key to reading and understanding.

It reveals something of the mind of Paul to note that the subsections (chapters 12, 13 and 14) are themselves arranged in a concentric pattern. This yields a careful and subtle pattern across the whole text. The two questions to have in mind always are:

- Is the physical centre, the centre of meaning? (usually, yes).

- when the reader comes 'back' to A^1, what advance in argument has been made?

For example, when discussing prophetic gifts in chapter 12, he slips in a teaching about the Church being the body of Christ. And the teaching is balanced like this:

A	B	A^1
diversity	members	actual order
one God	one body	in the body of Christ

One could jump from A to A^1 because they belong together; they use the same language of charism, tongues and prophecy. But the choice of image can condition us to accept the description of the Church as an ordered and co-ordinated diversity. Hence the B section is not just a colourful illustration but contributes an essential element to the argument which is taken up in 12:31b. Such movement can be found across all three chapters here:

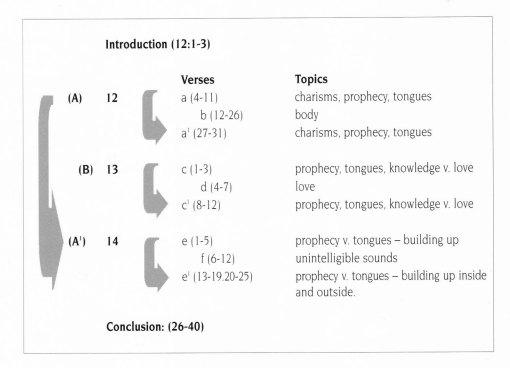

		Verses	**Topics**
(A)	**12**	a (4-11)	charisms, prophecy, tongues
		b (12-26)	body
		a¹ (27-31)	charisms, prophecy, tongues
(B)	**13**	c (1-3)	prophecy, tongues, knowledge v. love
		d (4-7)	love
		c¹ (8-12)	prophecy, tongues, knowledge v. love
(A¹)	**14**	e (1-5)	prophecy v. tongues – building up
		f (6-12)	unintelligible sounds
		e¹ (13-19.20-25)	prophecy v. tongues – building up inside and outside.

Introduction (12:1-3)

Conclusion: (26-40)

b) A Comment on the Overview

Introduction (12:1-3): Paul begins with an affirmation which must be read against the background of the Corinthians' conversion and the gifts of the Holy Spirit. This positive opening leads eventually to the discernment of gifts in chapter 14.

a. (4-11): In itself, this is a quite poetic passage with careful repetition and rhythm. Paul affirms diversity but does so immediately and inseparably in the context of unity – unity around the Spirit, the Lord, God. To offset any personal merit in the gifts, he insists that the author and giver of the gifts is the Holy Spirit.

b. (12-26) The body needs parts to be a body: Paul here does not mean the '*mystical* body' (an expression not found in Paul), but simply the actual body of believers. He means that you cannot love without mutuality. The body is the body because of the harmony of the parts.

a¹. (27-31) Paul then illustrates how the Church is articulated by the variety of functions within the community. Rhetorical questions are used to question the glamour gifts. A and A' belong together, dealing with gifts; the imagery of the body already anticipates the criterion which is going to come up again in chapter 14 on the building up of the Church. But before he comes to that application he wants to ground that criterion in the highest Christian gift, which is love. Hence, he states exactly what is the nature of the cohesion of the Christian body.

c. (13:1-3) The negative case for love: Paul means, literally, *nothing*, and that is important for his persuasion. At the end of verse 3 he inserts a word which will become important as part of the criterion for distinguishing tongues and prophecy: 'I *gain* nothing'. The gain for the community will be the criterion for putting tongues below prophecy in the church's life.

d. (13:4-7) Here Paul moves from the mode of negative comparison to positive praise. This eulogy (or *elogium*) will be seen in greater detail below.

c¹. (13:8-13) The point of comparison here is that the gifts all fail, but faith, hope and love do not. Even within these highest gifts there is an ascending order, making love the greatest gift of all. He repeats this negatively by making a comparison between perfect and imperfect, and by using the ages of man as

He means that you cannot love without mutuality.

The gain for the community will be the criterion for putting tongues below prophecy in the church's life.

The gifts all fail.

a mirror. He then comes to that mysterious statement, 'I shall know even as I am known'. Paul has in this section shown that there *is* a gradation in the gifts within the Church. Simply, the highest is love.

e. (14:1-5) Paul begins the evaluation of, and comparison between, prophecy and tongues. He establishes a criterion already hinted at in the comparison about the body – what is good is good for the whole body. He will go on to show that prophecy is more important for the whole body than tongues. That is his point.

f. (14:6-12) Here, the criterion is applied: Of what use will the gift be? Paul then uses a threefold comparison based on sounds, whether they are intelligible or unintelligible: harp/flute; a trumpet in war; or speaking with a foreigner. Unless the message is clear and understood, the effort would be pointless. He has already anticipated the comparison with sounds (13:1-3) by using the image of the clanging cymbal or an echoing bronze.

e'. (14:13-19, 20-25) A careful distinction is made between prophecy and tongues. Tongues make an impression on outsiders, but prophecy builds up the members. Again, if someone should visit the assembly, would the visitor not be more likely to be built up by prophecy and its clear explanation, than by tongues and the attendant confusion?

Tongues make an impression on outsiders, but prophecy builds up the members.

Conclusion. (14:26-40) Finally, Paul draws out the practical conclusions. It may be worth noting that the section on women speaking at worship is almost certainly a later interpolation in the text and not part of Paul's original teaching. There are four reasons for this.

The section on women speaking at worship is almost certainly a later interpolation in the text and not part of Paul's original teaching.

- Firstly, women in worship was not an issue in verses 12-14, but tongues and prophecies are.
- Secondly, if the reader passes from verse 33 directly to verse 37, the reading is seamless and coherent.
- Thirdly, it contradicts Paul's practice of having women deacons, evangelists and apostles, as found in Romans 16.
- Fourthly, it contradicts Paul's principle that in Christ, 'there is no longer Jew or Greek, there is no longer slave or free, there is no longer male and female; for all of you are one in Christ Jesus. And if you belong to Christ, then you are Abraham's offspring, heirs according to the promise' (Gal 3:28-29).

EXERCISE 7:

a) *What were the problems in Corinthian worship as shown by 1 Corinthians 12-14? Write 5 lines.*

b) *How is the centrality of love expressed in 1 Corinthians 12-14? Write 5 lines.*

The next part of this unit deals with 1 *Corinthians* 13 from the point of view of classical rhetoric, and specifically from the aspect of *genre*. There were three possible *genres* in classical rhetoric:

- forensic (courtroom);
- deliberative (politics); and
- epideictic (celebratory).

It seems clear that 1 *Corinthians* 13 does not much resemble a political speech or a courtroom defence. The *genre*, therefore, seems to be celebratory rhetoric (Latin: *genus demonstrativum*). Paul actually uses the word 'show' or 'demonstrate' in the very first verse (12:31).

2.   1 CORINTHIANS 13

2.1   SUBDIVISIONS

Careful delimitation of 1 *Corinthians* 13 yields several subdivisions. The passage opens with an introduction (12:31) and closes with a conclusion (13:13). There is a frame using the words 'greater' and 'greatest'.

Part One: 13:1-3

The rhetorical 'I' is the subject. Notice the unfolding in three sentences (or periods) and the parallelism.

> [1]If I speak in the tongues of mortals and of angels, but do not have love, I am a noisy gong or a clanging cymbal. [2]And if I have prophetic powers, and understand all mysteries and all knowledge, and if I have all faith, so as to remove mountains, but do not have love, I am nothing. [3]If I give away all my possessions, and if I hand over my body so that I may boast, but do not have love, I gain nothing. (1 Cor 13:1-3)

Part Two: 13:4-7

In these few verses, there are no fewer than fifteen verbs in the third person singular. The use of the word 'all" creates a climax at the end.

> [4]Love is patient; love is kind; love is not envious or boastful or arrogant [5]or rude. It does not insist on its own way; it is not irritable or resentful; [6]it does not rejoice in wrongdoing, but rejoices in the truth. [7]It bears all things, believes all things, hopes all things, endures all things. (1 Cor 13:4-7)

Part Three: 13:8-12

In this section, 'we' alternates with 'I'. There are repeated antitheses held together in a chronological frame moving from 'then' to 'now'.

> [8]Love never ends. But as for prophecies, they will come to an end; as for tongues, they will cease; as for knowledge, it will come to an end. [9]For we know only in part, and we prophesy only in part; [10]but when the complete comes, the partial will come to an end. [11]When I was a child, I spoke like a child, I thought like a child, I reasoned like a child; when I became an adult, I put an end to childish ways. [12]For now we see in a mirror, dimly, but then we will see face to face. Now I know only in part; then I will know fully, even as I have been fully known. (1 Cor 13:8-12)

Conclusion: 13:13

Here, the inclusion with 12:13 can be seen.

> [13]And now faith, hope, and love abide, these three; and the greatest of these is love. (1 Cor 13:13)

2.2 THE LITERARY STYLE OF THE PASSAGE

In the rhetorical handbooks, the difference between forensic and deliberative, on the one hand, and celebratory is, in part, that the celebratory appeals not by argument as such, but by pleasing and entertaining the audience. It was especially recommended to use

- unusual words (new words, old-fashioned words and metaphors);
- balanced sentences;
- antithesis;
- repetition of words and expressions; and
- rhythm.

All of these are very present in this passage.

It is noticeable as well that Paul personifies love. This is a key to the passage, because the celebratory rhetoric (Latin: *genus demonstrativum*) was especially suited for praising people, their qualities, characters, backgrounds and achievements. In particular, speakers could start with external circumstances, move on through physical attributes and climax with the qualities of character exhibited. In this vein,

Paul personifies love

- Part One deals with practical knowledge of languages and intellectual faculties.

- Part Two elaborates the virtues of temperance, justice and courage. And finally,

- Part Three (arranged in chronological sequences) traces the evolution and lasting dimensions of love.

A subtlety of this personification is that one can easily place oneself in the place of love, and so measure oneself against the vision offered here.

The primacy of love, shown by negative comparison

If I speak in the tongues of men and of angels,
    but have not love,
        I *am a noisy gong or a clanging cymbal.*

And if I have prophetic powers,
and understand all mysteries and all knowledge,
and if I have all faith,
so as to remove mountains,
    but have not love,
        I *am nothing.*

If I give away all I have,
and if I deliver my body to be burned,
    but have not love,
        I *gain nothing.*

The character of love

Love is patient and kind;
love is not jealous or boastful; it is not arrogant or rude;
love does not insist on its own way; it is not irritable or resentful.
it does not rejoice at wrong, but rejoices in the right.

Love   bears all things,
        believes all things,
        hopes all things,
        endures all things.

The permanence of love, shown by comparison

Love never ends;
as for prophecies,   they will pass away;
as for tongues,   they will cease;
as for knowledge,   it will pass away.

For our knowledge is   imperfect
and our prophecy is   imperfect;
But when the   perfect comes,
                          the imperfect will pass away.

When I was a child,   I spoke like a child,
                          I thought like a child;
When I became a man,   I gave up childish ways.

For now we see in a mirror dimly,
                          but then face to face.
Now I know in part;   then I shall understand fully,
                          even as I have been fully understood.

And so...
        Faith, hope, love abide, these three;
        but the greatest of these is love.

EXERCISE 8:

a) What are the literary features of I Corinthians 13? Write 5 lines.

b) What is the message of I Corinthians 13? Write 5 lines.

2.3   THE MESSAGE OF 1 CORINTHIANS 13

Love is patient, love is kind

These are the necessary passive and active characteristics of love, portraying forbearance and active generosity. They are incidentally the characteristics of God's attitude to us as understood in Pauline theology. There then follow seven verbs showing how love does not behave; the first five would appear to be pointed references to the Corinthian situation.

Love does not envy

Oddly, this verb is usually positive in Paul (see 14:1). But it occurs in 1 Corinthians 3:3 to denote strife and rivalry. Believers shouldn't be in competition – especially over those who 'merely' bring them the good news.

Love does not boast

The key word here means literally 'to be a braggart or a windbag'. It may refer to those who desire the more flashy gifts of the Spirit. Or perhaps it refers to those who think they have a special wisdom not given to others, which makes them feel superior. It breaks the harmony of the community: it is not possible to love and to boast at the same time.

It is not possible to love and to boast at the same time.

Love is not proud

Again, the verb means literally 'to be puffed up'. It is a word rarely used in the New Testament, found only once outside 1 Corinthians (Col 2:18). In 1 Corinthians it is used exclusively to describe the Corinthians themselves, especially in opposition to Paul (4:6,18-19; 5:2 and 8:1).

Love is not rude

The key word here means 'to act shamefully'. Perhaps it refers to those who dress in such a way as to obscure the distinction between the sexes (11:2-16) or to the well-off people who were making the poor feel uncomfortable at the Lord's Supper.

Love is not self-seeking

Before insisting on one's rights, one should ask what good one can do for one's brother or sister (see 10:24.33).

Love is not easily angered

This actually means 'to provoke someone'. This is an extension of the forbearance mentioned at the beginning.

Love does not keep a record of wrongs

God does not keep a reckoning against us, and we should not keep a reckoning against others.

Love does not delight in evil, but rejoices in the truth.

The thought broadens out to the gospel and all that is opposed to it; love is never perniciously glad when misfortune befalls another.

Love bears all things, believes all things, hopes all things, endures all things.

Here, Paul becomes quite rhapsodic about the qualities of love.

Paul has identified love as the highest gift. The Corinthians, competitive in their believing, were eager to know and to have the highest gift. The surprising thing is that love, the highest gift of all, was not only given to some, but to all. Paul thereby undermines spiritual pride and self-satisfaction.

2.4   THE RELATIONSHIP TO JESUS' TEACHING

Elsewhere in his letters, Paul names love as the highest practice.

> Owe no one anything, except to love one another; for the one who loves another has fulfilled the law. (Rom 13:8)

> Love does no wrong to a neighbour; therefore, love is the fulfilling of the law. (Rom 13:10)

> For the whole law is summed up in a single commandment, 'You shall love your neighbour as yourself.' (Gal 5:14)

Anyone familiar with the gospels will not fail to notice the link with Jesus' own teaching as exemplified in *Mark* 12.

> One of the scribes came near and heard them disputing with one another, and seeing that he answered them well, he asked him, 'Which commandment is the first of all?' Jesus answered, 'The first is, "Hear, O Israel: the Lord our God, the Lord is one; you shall love the Lord your God with all your heart, and with all your soul, and with all your mind, and with all your strength." The second is this, "You shall love your neighbor as yourself." There is no other commandment greater than these.' Then the scribe said to him, 'You are right, Teacher; you have truly said that "he is one, and besides him there is no other"; and "to love him with all the heart, and with all the understanding, and with all the strength," and "to love one's neighbor as oneself," – this is much more important than all whole burnt offerings and sacrifices.' When Jesus saw that he answered wisely, he said to him, 'You are not far from the kingdom of God.' After that no one dared to ask him any question. (Mk 12:28-34)

3.   CONCLUSION

It would have been possible for Paul to have given simple practical instructions on how to resolve the issues causing difficulty in the Corinthian assemblies. But this was not Paul's way. Again and again, Paul put before his hearers and readers the deeper thinking behind his practical advice, so that when the advice was finally given, it was obvious that it was grounded in some core Christian value. This was true as never before in 1 *Corinthians* 12-14.

 Benedict XVI: Deus Caritas Est *n.18*

Love of God and love of neighbour are thus inseparable, they form a single commandment. But both live from the love of God who has loved us first. No longer is it a question, then, of a 'commandment' imposed from without and calling for the impossible, but rather of a freely-bestowed experience of love from within, a love which by its very nature must then be shared with others. Love grows through love. Love is 'divine' because it comes from God and unites us to God; through this unifying process it makes us a 'we' which transcends our divisions and makes us one, until in the end God is 'all in all' (1 Cor 15:28).

EXERCISE 9:

a) *Describe Paul's theology of love. Write 5 lines.*

b) *What are the links between Paul's teaching and that of Jesus? Write 5 lines.*

SECTION FIVE:

THE RESURRECTION

(1 CORINTHIANS 15)

Fig. 12: *The Resurrection*

I. INTRODUCTION

The question of the end of life is one that touches everybody. This is as true of us today as it was for St Paul's Corinthians. Of course, throughout his writings, Paul teaches the resurrection of Jesus from the dead; and even when this is not the direct topic under discussion, it is always there in the background for him and for his readers. There is a biographical context for this: it was his own encounter with the risen Lord which turned the life of 'Paul the Pharisee' right around.

The passage in 1 *Corinthians* 15 is Paul's most sustained reflection on the resurrection of Jesus, and also of all believers in him. A note of caution may be in order here. When reading 1 *Corinthians* 15 first, one might have the impression that somehow Paul was trying to prove the reality of Jesus' resurrection; but this is actually not the case. To anticipate somewhat, Paul presumed a shared faith in the resurrection and goes on to draw out the consequences of this for the future resurrection of the dead, in Christ. This is really the topic of 1 *Corinthians* 15.

Was Paul was trying to prove the reality of Jesus' resurrection?

2.   THE PROBLEM AT CORINTH

Students will remember from the earlier study of 1 *Thessalonians* that the members of the church there were anxious about those who had already died and who would not 'be around' when the Lord returned at the Second Coming. The Corinthians' problem was somewhat different, though perhaps related. They cannot imagine that the dead will be raised, and they are tempted to think that once you are dead, you are dead. This is not such a strange idea. For most of the Old Testament period, people believed in a God for this life only, and it was only very late in the Hebrew Bible that the beginnings of a faith in life after death began to emerge. Furthermore, for Greek culture, with its sharp awareness of decay and death, there was a kind of dismissal of the body in favour of the spiritual principle within, the soul. This was not exactly the problem in Corinth, as far as can be seen, but the irreversibility of death and the impossibility of a resurrection of this body had certainly played a part in shaping the attitudes of the Corinthians as good Greeks. Today, perhaps, with the weakening of orthodox faith, people have more sympathy with the Corinthians. Contemporary people tend to believe more in a God for this life, and cannot really imagine that there might be more.

3.   THE CHALLENGES PAUL FACED

3.1   RESURRECTION

Any real continuity would be through your offspring in this world.

shade

pit

sheol

As noted above, for much of the Old Testament period, there was no real teaching on life after death; it was simply accepted that death was natural, and any real continuity would be through one's offspring in this world. They did imagine that the 'shade' of the dead person – not exactly one's soul and not really one's full self either – had a kind of shadowy subsistence in the underworld. There are a variety of names for this 'place', such as 'the Pit', but the most generally used name was 'Sheol'. It would be wrong to overestimate the significance of Sheol because it was accepted that as the bones of a dead person were placed underground, something of the person went down there too. There was nothing more to that belief. There were one or two striking exceptions to this – such as Elijah who went to heaven in a fiery chariot (2 Kings 2:11), and Enoch (Gen 5:23) whom God took. It should be noted that the language of resurrection only entered the Bible courtesy of Ezekiel who wrote graphically of a type of resurrection in the vision of the dead bones (Ezek 37). However, it is clear that Ezekiel's meaning is thoroughly metaphorical, and he was speaking not of the resurrection of dead bodies but of a future 'resurrection' of Israel in the generations after the Exile.

By the first century ce, the Pharisees and many others believed firmly in the resurrection of the dead.

There is quite a contrast between the teaching just described and the belief of many Jews at the time of Jesus. By the first century ce, the Pharisees and many others believed firmly in the resurrection of the dead. For instance, such a belief is presumed in *Mark* 12. What had happened in the intervening years and centuries for such a striking development to have taken place? Two contexts help explain the relatively quick and substantial development of a doctrine of the resurrection of the dead. The first was persecution, and the second was apocalyptic.

It is not an accident that the first mention of a real resurrection of the dead in the Hebrew Bible comes in the the *Book of Daniel*, reflecting a time of intense persecution.

At that time Michael, the great prince, the protector of your people, shall arise. There shall be a time of anguish, such as has never occurred since nations first came into existence. But at that time your people shall be delivered, everyone who is found written in the book. Many of those who sleep in the dust of the earth shall awake, some to everlasting life, and some to shame and everlasting contempt. Those who are wise shall shine like the brightness of the sky, and those who lead many to righteousness, like the stars forever and ever. But you, Daniel, keep the words secret and the book sealed until the time of the end. Many shall be running back and forth, and evil shall increase. (Dan 12:11-14)

The *Book of Daniel* was written at a time of persecution under Antiochus IV Epiphanes (c.215-164 bce). He was king of Syria from 175 to 164 bce. Antiochus instigated considerable change in Jerusalem and in Jewish religious practices. He brought Greek culture to Jerusalem in the form of civic architecture – such as a gymnasium where athletes took part unclothed. He tried to replace the Torah (the Law) with new laws. He also tried to establish a new order of worship in the Temple, involving worship of 'the Lord of heaven' (the Semitic, *Baal Shamin*). This latter idolatry was called by Jewish writers of the period the 'desolating sacrilege' or the 'abomination of desolation' (see Dan 11:31;12:11; 1 Macc 1:54; Mt 24:15; Mk 13:14).

Fig. 13: *Antiochus* IV

The imposition of the new order triggered a rebellion which was first centred around the Maccabean (or Hasmonean) family, led by Mattathias, a priest of Modein, and then by his sons Judas, Jonathan and Simon in turn. The reaction of the government was persecution, as can be read in 1 *and* 2 *Maccabees*.

The persecution created an acute religious problem for the Jews. Until this time, they believed God to be just and to act justly towards his faithful in this life. They held this belief, even in the face of considerable evidence to the contrary (see Psalms 37 and 73). However, martyrdom constituted an extreme example of religious fidelity and by definition there would be no chance of any reward for a martyr in this life. And so, in order to continue to speak of God as just, the horizons of faith were expanded to include a doctrine of life after death. Significantly, it was predicated upon God as creator. A moving passage from 2 *Maccabees* – an arresting story of a mother with her seven sons – illustrates the point:

In order to continue to speak of God as just, the horizons of faith were expanded to include a doctrine of life after death.

> The mother was especially admirable and worthy of honourable memory. Although she saw her seven sons perish within a single day, she bore it with good courage because of her hope in the Lord. She encouraged each of them in the language of their ancestors. Filled with a noble spirit, she reinforced her woman's reasoning with a man's courage, and said to them, 'I do not know how you came into being in my womb. It was not I who gave you life and breath, nor I who set in order the elements within each of you. Therefore the Creator of the world, who shaped the beginning of humankind and devised the origin of all things, will in his mercy give life and breath back to you again, since you now forget yourselves for the sake of his laws.' (2 Macc 7:20-23)

Intimately connected to the question of fidelity under persecution was the evolution of a worldview and a literary form known as apocalyptic. In a general way, the apocalyptic worldview teaches that present sufferings – usually threatening to religious and cultural identity – are only the latest manifestation of evil. This is experienced by believers because they live 'in this present evil age'. However, a new age is about to dawn. This 'age to come' will be inaugurated by the Day of Lord, a day on which God will reassert his rule at the end of history, punishing the wicked and rewarding the good. In that future transformation, all

apocalyptic

They believed in the resurrection of the dead.

the injustices undergone by the faithful, all the innocent suffering, all the faithfulness under pressure will be rewarded by a new life with God, beyond history. The word for this transformed life is 'resurrection'. Thus they did not mean simply that the dead would be alive again, nor did they believe simply in the immortality of the soul. Instead, they believed in the resurrection of the dead. To capture this sense of the unknown, certain lines from St Paul can help:

> But, as it is written, 'What no eye has seen, nor ear heard, nor the human heart conceived, what God has prepared for those who love him' – these things God has revealed to us through the Spirit; for the Spirit searches everything, even the depths of God. (1 Cor 2:9-11)

This captures the sense of the 'beyond' of the resurrection perfectly. The foundational metaphor for the resurrection is 'to wake up'. Just as when I am asleep and when I am awake I am the same person, and so it will be at the resurrection of the dead, I will be myself. But also, just as when I am asleep and when I am awake, there is a very considerable difference in my mode of being. This is how it will be at the resurrection of the dead because everyone will be utterly transformed. Thus the metaphor of 'rising' conveys the essential continuity and discontinuity of resurrection.

Finally, it was part of the apocalyptic worldview that there would be a congruence between the end and the beginning which would in some sense resemble each other. This is presumed by the mother in the story above, who bases her faith on God as creator, who can and will take those faithful to him across the bar of death. It was also presumed by St Paul when he spoke of Christ as the Second Adam. It may very well be, of course, that Paul's Corinthians appreciated nothing of this deep background and subtle teaching.

3.2   IMAGINATION

As will be noted below, Paul's first step in persuading the Corinthians is rather logical: if there is no resurrection of the dead, that is, none whatsoever, then logically Christ cannot be raised. It is equally important to notice that the second persuasion is an attempt to expand the religious imagination of the Corinthians, so that they would be able to see, however unclearly what kind of bodies might the transformed, risen bodies be? In the first argument Paul tried to show that belief in the resurrection of Jesus entailed belief in our resurrection too. In the second argument, Paul set about destabilising the univocal understanding of 'body' so as to open up their minds and hearts to other ways of being body, ways other than the literal resuscitation of a corpse. He moved from the 'what' of our resurrection to the 'how'.

3.3   PAUL'S APPROACH

The approach that Paul takes in 1 *Corinthians* 15 combines several dimensions.

- Firstly, Paul shares with the Corinthians a faith in Jesus as raised from the dead. This is foundational, and expresses a shared world.

- Secondly, Paul offers the Corinthians some logic, along the lines just indicated. If Christ is risen, then there has been at least one resurrection. The series of logical questions is quite impressive.

- However, logic takes Paul only so far. The real motor behind what he says is his apocalyptic worldview, and so, thirdly, as the centre of each of his persuasions in 1 *Corinthians* 15, is an unabashed apocalyptic faith in God and his Christ as the New Adam.

This three-pronged attack may help to keep track of what Paul is saying in 1 *Corinthians* 15.

4.   CONCENTRIC PATTERNS

It has been noted before that sometimes Paul's arguments fall into concentric patterns, such as ABA[1]. This happens to an intriguing degree in 1 *Corinthians* 15.

After some introductory material (which will be explored below), the arguments of 1 *Corinthians* 15 can be divided into two parts.

- First of all, there is the logical argument, along the lines indicated above, taking in verses 13-25. These fall into the following pattern:

  A   13-19   Logical incoherence – style: questions.
  B   20-28   Adam and Christ as prototypes.
  A[1]   29-34   Practical incoherence – style: questions.

- In the second place, the argument about the 'how' of the resurrection also falls into a concentric pattern:

  C   36-44   Varieties of bodies
  D   45-49   The first Adam and the last Adam as prototypes
  C[1]   50-56   The change which is the resurrected body.

4.1   THE LOGICAL PERSUASION

1 *Corinthians* 15:13-25

In the logical persuasion, the outer sections resemble each other in language and thought.

A 'Pure' logic	A[1] Practical logic
[13]*If there is no resurrection of the dead*, then Christ has not been raised; [14]and *if Christ has not been raised*, then our proclamation has been in vain and your faith has been in vain. [15]We are even found to be misrepresenting God, because we testified of God that he raised Christ – whom he did not raise if it is true that the dead are not raised. [16]For *if the dead are not raised*, then Christ has not been raised. [17]*If Christ has not been raised*, your faith is futile and you are still in your sins. [18]Then those also who have died in Christ have perished. [19]*If for this life only we have hoped in Christ*, we are of all people most to be pitied.	[29]Otherwise, what will those people do who receive baptism on behalf of the dead? *If the dead are not raised at all*, why are people baptised on their behalf? [30]And why are we putting ourselves in danger every hour? [31]I die every day! That is as certain, brothers and sisters, as my boasting of you – a boast that I make in Christ Jesus our Lord. [32]*If with merely human hopes I fought with wild animals at Ephesus*, what would I have gained by it? *If the dead are not raised*, "Let us eat and drink, for tomorrow we die."

The opening sentence in A contains the key, the first link in an inexorable chain of argument. It is in a sense 'pure' logic, drawing out the purely logical consequences of the passage. Of itself, it may not yet move hearts. The logic in A[1] is of a different order, being more practical. It is a 'why bother' argument. Why should the community practise baptism on behalf of the dead if the dead are not raised? Why should Paul risk his life regularly for the gospel if the gospel is for now only? Why should we not all relax and enjoy ourselves because this is all there is? These are good practical questions which may indeed move hearts.

The puzzling mention of baptism on behalf of the dead can surprise readers today. The background may be something like this. Let us imagine a woman from Corinth who has come to believe in Christ, has undergone a conversion, and now lives in faith, hope and love. The discovery of the treasure of the faith may cause dismay that people close to her, who have already died, never came to this realisation. One could think, perhaps, of a child or a parent. In order to associate some dear departed one with the hope she now has in Christ, baptism on behalf of the dead was offered. Paul neither approves nor disapproves. At this point of the argument, it is sufficient that concern for the dead should include this practice which would make no sense if the dead were not raised. In any case, the resemblance of A and A¹ is clear enough. The central section B will be looked at below.

4.2 THE EXPANSION OF IMAGINATION

1 Corinthians 15:36-56

Again, in the expansion of imagination, the outer sections resemble each other in language and thought.

C 'Science' argument for variety	**C¹ Faith argument for transformation**
³⁶Fool! What you sow does not come to life unless it dies. ³⁷And as for what you sow, you do not sow the *body* that is to be, but a bare seed, perhaps of wheat or of some other grain. ³⁸But God gives it a *body* as he has chosen, and to each kind of seed its own *body*. ³⁹Not all *flesh* is alike, but there is one *flesh* for human beings, another for animals, another for birds, and another for fish. ⁴⁰There are both heavenly *bodies* and earthly *bodies*, but the glory of the heavenly is one thing, and that of the earthly is another. ⁴¹There is one glory of the sun, and another glory of the moon, and another glory of the stars; indeed, star differs from star in glory. ⁴²So it is with <u>the resurrection of the dead</u>. What is sown is *perishable*, what is raised is *imperishable*. ⁴³It is sown in dishonour, it is raised in glory. It is sown in weakness, it is raised in power. ⁴⁴It is sown a *physical body*, it is raised a *spiritual body*. If there is a *physical body*, there is also a *spiritual body*.	⁵⁰What I am saying, brothers and sisters, is this: *flesh* and *blood* cannot inherit the kingdom of God, nor does the *perishable* inherit the *imperishable*. ⁵¹Listen, I will tell you a mystery! <u>We will not all die, but we will all be changed</u>, ⁵²in a moment, in the twinkling of an eye, at the last trumpet. For the trumpet will sound, and the dead will be raised *imperishable*, and we will be changed. ⁵³For this *perishable body* must put on *imperishability*, and this *mortal body* must put on *immortality*. ⁵⁴When this *perishable body* puts on *imperishability*, and this *mortal body* puts on *immortality*, then the saying that is written will be fulfilled: "Death has been swallowed up in victory." ⁵⁵"Where, O death, is your victory? Where, O death, is your sting?" ⁵⁶The sting of death is sin, and the power of sin is the law.

In the first section C, Paul tries to show from nature that 'body' can mean a great variety of things, from a tree to a fish to a planet. He combines that observation with farming imagery which speaks of the transformation (death) of the seed which grows into something quite different (the body). Thus, he teaches that what we mean by body now may not be at all like the resurrected body in the future. 'Spiritual body' is a new term, invented by Paul, as a way holding on to his own Jewish background which thinks of the human being as a single body with spirit. Second C¹ builds on that destabilising of a single meaning of body to include the transformed, resurrected body when 'we will all be changed'. Paul does not claim to know what that will be like. It is enough for him that Jesus already shares in this future life which 'God has prepared for those who love him'.

Of course the previous pattern AA¹ and the current pattern CC¹ are logical enough, and could be perceived at least in principle even by people with no faith. But why should one think all of this is a reality? Logic and (improved) imagination are not enough for the core argument about whether all this is true or not. Instead, Paul makes use of his apocalyptic worldview in the central sections of his persuasion.

4.3 APOCALYPTIC SECTIONS

1 Corinthians 15:20-29, 45-49

Once more, as one looks at these sections, it is apparent that the central moments B and D resemble each other in language and thought.

B The sequence of the end	**D The transformation of the end**
²⁰But in fact Christ has been raised from the dead, the first fruits of those who have died. ²¹For *since death came through a human being, the resurrection of the dead has also come through a human being;* ²²for *as all die in Adam,* so all will be made alive in Christ. ²³But each in his own order: Christ the first fruits, then at his coming those who belong to Christ. ²⁴Then comes the end, when he hands over the kingdom to God the Father, after he has destroyed every ruler and every authority and power. ²⁵For he must reign until he has put all his enemies under his feet. ²⁶The last enemy to be destroyed is death. ²⁷For 'God has put all things in subjection under his feet.' But when it says, "All things are put in subjection," it is plain that this does not include the one who put all things in subjection under him. ²⁸When all things are subjected to him, then the Son himself will also be subjected to the one who put all things in subjection under him, so that God may be all in all.	⁴⁵Thus it is written, '*The first man, Adam, became a living being*'; the last Adam became a life-giving spirit. ⁴⁶But it is not the spiritual that is first, but the physical, and then the spiritual. ⁴⁷*The first man was from the earth, a man of dust;* the second man is from heaven. ⁴⁸As *was the man of dust, so are those who are of the dust;* and as is the man of heaven, so are those who are of heaven. ⁴⁹*Just as we have borne the image of the man of dust,* we will also bear the image of the man of heaven.

In the first section, B, the conviction that the beginning and the end should resemble each other guides the underlying thought. Adam was one person; Christ is one person. All die in Adam; all will be made alive in Christ. These are faith convictions expressed in apocalyptic language. The rather longer section starting in verse 23 is also quite apocalyptic. Because the apocalyptic imagination was dealing with history and with the present evil age and the age to come, there was lively interest in the sequence and final unfolding of God's purpose.

These are faith convictions expressed in apocalyptic language.

Paul, like all early Christians, believed that the end had already started with Jesus' resurrection. But complete victory would not be achieved until the very end of time. That is why Paul was careful to say, in verse 26, that the last enemy to be destroyed is death. Such a teaching is aimed directly at the concerns of the Corinthians. E*ven though Christ is raised*, people still experience death because death is the last enemy to be destroyed. And *because death is the last enemy to be destroyed*, the human race has hope for those already dead. Continuing in a very apocalyptic vein, in section D, Paul goes back to the parallel between Adam and Christ. Although the balancing of 'faith statements' may seem artificial, nevertheless the pairing of Adam and Christ follows the pattern of the mother of the seven sons in 2 *Maccabees*. The creator brought us into being starting with Adam, the man of dust. The creator will also bring us into the new creation starting with Christ, the man of heaven. The end will resemble the beginning, only far more wonderfully.

Because logic and imagination can only take us so far, Paul has to reach out to the deep convictions of the Corinthians who shared his faith in Christ. Because Christ is raised, all this is not just something possible, but real. The reality of it is amplified and expressed using the language of Paul's own religious background, apocalyptic. His audience in Corinth is certainly mixed, and it is a moot point to what extent they would have understood and shared his vision. To help them grasp the reality in the idiom of their own culture, all of this persuasion follows the rules of conventional rhetoric.

5.   RHETORICAL STRUCTURE

The pattern discovered above helps in following the overall argument of 1 *Corinthians* 15.

Rhetoric	Verses	Sequence	Topic
Introduction	1-2		Wish to inform them, lest they believe in vain.
Statement of Facts	3-11		Creed, appearances, Paul's conversion
Proof 1	12	Thesis	If Christ is raised then there is a resurrection
	13-19	A	No resurrection would mean no risen Christ
	20-28	B	Adam and Christ compared
	29-34	A¹	If there is no resurrection, what is the point of it all?
Proof 2	35	Thesis	How are the dead raised?
	36-44	C	Body has many meanings
	45-49	D	Adam and Christ compared
	50-56	C¹	The mystery of the bodily resurrection
Conclusion	57		Be steadfast, lest in vain.

5.1   THE INTRODUCTION

> ¹Now I would remind you, brothers and sisters, of the good news that I proclaimed to you, which you in turn received, in which also you stand, ²through which also you are being saved, if you hold firmly to the message that I proclaimed to you– unless you have come to believe in vain. (1 Cor 15:1-2)

The introduction had to achieve three things:

- to get people's attention;
- to win their good will; and
- to make them receptive.

It is probable that Paul had already been informed of the Corinthians' questions and difficulties about the resurrection. The list of qualities is reassuring and at the same time destabilising:

The reminder of Paul's evangelisation should indeed remind them of their original good-will towards Paul. Their present benefit is stated in summary form: 'in which you stand, through which also you are being saved'. An upsetting possibility comes into play in the final qualifiers: 'if' and 'unless'. These very probably provoke them to ask what does he mean? At least, it should trigger their attention.

5.2 THE STATEMENT OF FACTS

³For I handed on to you as of first importance what I in turn had received: that Christ died for our sins in accordance with the scriptures, ⁴and that he was buried, and that he was raised on the third day in accordance with the scriptures, ⁵and that he appeared to Cephas, then to the twelve. ⁶Then he appeared to more than five hundred brothers and sisters at one time, most of whom are still alive, though some have died. ⁷Then he appeared to James, then to all the apostles. ⁸Last of all, as to one untimely born, he appeared also to me. ⁹For I am the least of the apostles, unfit to be called an apostle, because I persecuted the church of God. ¹⁰But by the grace of God I am what I am, and his grace toward me has not been in vain. On the contrary, I worked harder than any of them – though it was not I, but the grace of God that is with me. ¹¹Whether then it was I or they, so we proclaim and so you have come to believe. (1 Cor 15:3-11)

It is vital to be clear on what Paul was achieving here. He was reminding them of their fundamental faith in Christ risen from the dead, before going on to draw out the consequence that, in Christ, the dead too will rise. In order to remind them of what they genuinely already believed, Paul started with a type of creed (somewhat adjusted) in verses 3-5. He then went on to list the appearances of the risen Lord, modestly including himself at the end of the list, as the 'least of the apostles'. The important point is the shared conviction of the first believers – Paul and the Corinthians themselves. Christ's resurrection stands at the heart of what they believe. This needs to be established before going on to the logical arguments in verses 12-34 and the imagination arguments in verses 35-56. So, this paragraph corresponds to the 'statement of facts' in speech-making, that is, the information accepted by all sides before going on to argue further or draw out the faith consequences.

In Christ, the dead too will rise.

6. THE TEACHING

Paul shared with the first believers and with the Corinthians a deep faith in Christ risen from the dead. The difficulty of the Corinthians stemmed from the fact of death and the decay of the body. They could not imagine that there should be a bodily life with God after death. Paul tried to show that their position was both illogical and hopeless. It was illogical because they seemed to be saying that there was no resurrection of the dead at all – a stance which would exclude even Jesus' resurrection. It was also hopeless because, if our hope is for this life only, we are truly deluded, and the apostolic zeal of Paul, who risked his life for the gospel, is also a delusion. This kind of argument has a shock value.

The imagination argument is really an attempt to expand horizons: 'body' does not have to mean just one kind of body, the one I have now. On the contrary, we see in nature a great variety of bodies, even heavenly bodies. The conviction that we will all experience a bodily resurrection does not mean that we will all come back, so to speak, as we were before. On the contrary, there will be a transformation comparable to that which happens to a seed which is planted in the ground and becomes something completely other – while somehow remaining itself. Paul does not really know how this will come about, except to say that Jesus' resurrection will be the cause of it; and this is a mystery!

Jesus' resurrection will be the cause of it; and it is a mystery!

7. CONCLUSION

The teaching in 1 *Corinthians* 15 is not unrelated to contemporary issues of belief in a personal resurrection. There may be a tendency nowadays to believe in a God for this life only. There may be many reasons for this – perhaps a failure to think through the consequence of believing in Jesus' resurrection, perhaps a more basic failure of imagination. The difficulty we have in imagining the next stage of life after death is understandable. The baby in the womb cannot imagine its future, and yet there is an inevitable transition, called birth, which brings the baby to the next level of life. Adults are the same: one cannot imagine what life will be like after death. However, by being 'born-again' in Christ we believe our death will be a transition, a new birth into the new creation in Christ.

> So if anyone is in Christ, there is a new creation: everything old has passed away; see, everything has become new! (2 Cor 5:17)

> For neither circumcision nor uncircumcision is anything; but a new creation is everything! (Gal 6:15)

EXERCISE 10:

a) What difficulties did the Corinthians have about the resurrection? Write 5 lines.

b) Explain Paul's approach to the resurrection in either:

i.   1 Corinthians 15:12-34; or

ii.   1 Corinthians 15:35-56. Write 5 lines.

SECTION SIX:
PAUL AND MONEY

2 Corinthians 8-9

1. INTRODUCTION

In this section, a very practical side to Paul shall be seen. In 2 *Corinthians* 8-9, he appeals to the Corinthians to join in his collection for the churches in Judea. It is always a delicate thing to ask people for money. Two questions arise immediately. Firstly, why should one give at all? Secondly, why should one give to this venture and to these people? The manner in which Paul confronts these two arguments will be seen in detail and, in the course of the presentation, another side of Paul will emerge: Paul the administrator with a special emphasis on that modern virtue, transparency. The apostle was well capable of putting together a respectable team to administer the collection, and even saw to it that he himself was not directly involved, in case anyone should think that the funds might be diverted elsewhere.

At the same time, chapters 8 and 9, in their appeal and confidence, are an attempt to cement the relationship between Paul and the Corinthians. Thus he hopes to give concrete expression to their recent reconciliation.

2. PAUL AND MONEY

As can be seen from 1 Thessalonians, Paul does not like to take money from people for his personal support. In this, Paul follows rabbinic tradition according to which a rabbi ought to have a trade to support himself and not live from his work as a spiritual guide. It may also be the case that Paul has a somewhat middle-class attitude which made him slow to be indebted to those poorer than himself. He hesitates even to take money for the mission. It is clear, however, that he did, sometimes at least, accept donations.

A rabbi ought to have a trade to support himself and not live from his work as a spiritual guide.

I rejoice in the Lord greatly that now at last you have revived your concern for me; indeed, you were concerned for me, but had no opportunity to show it. Not that I am referring to being in need; for I have learned to be content with whatever I have. I know what it is to have little, and I know what it is to have plenty. In any and all circumstances I have learned the secret of being well-fed and of going hungry, of having plenty and of being in need. I can do all things through him who strengthens me. In any case, it was kind of you to share my distress. You Philippians indeed know that in the early days of the gospel, when I left Macedonia, no church shared with me in the matter of giving and receiving, except you alone. For even when I was in Thessalonica, you sent me help for my needs more than once. Not that I seek the gift, but I seek the profit that accumulates to your account. I have been paid in full and have more than enough; I am fully satisfied, now that I have received from Epaphroditus the gifts you sent, a fragrant offering, a sacrifice acceptable and pleasing to God. And my God will fully satisfy every need of yours according to his riches in glory in Christ Jesus. To our God and Father be glory forever and ever. Amen. (Phil 4:10-20)

3. THE COLLECTION

As is well known, Paul's mission was to the gentiles. But at the heart of his proclamation was a vision of both gentile and Jew in communion with each other in Christ. For him, as has been seen, the cross constituted the breaking down of the dividing wall, as *Ephesians* puts it.

> For he is our peace; in his flesh he has made both groups into one and has broken down the dividing wall, that is, the hostility between us. (Eph 2:14)

One of Paul's dreams was to bring to expression the union of Jew and gentile through a mutual exchange between both parts of the Christian movement. Broadly speaking, the gentiles have received everything from their Jewish fellow-believers, at least on a spiritual level. Paul hoped that some return might be made to the poorer Christians in Judea as an expression of gratitude, mutuality and communion. From the outset, it was envisioned as much more than a gift of money. It was to be a gesture of fellowship – a kind of sacramental or tangible way of making that fellowship a reality. The collection entailed a long story, reported in *Acts* and echoed in *Galatians*.

> At that time prophets came down from Jerusalem to Antioch. One of them named Agabus stood up and predicted by the Spirit that there would be a severe famine over all the world; and this took place during the reign of Claudius. The disciples determined that according to their ability, each would send relief to the believers living in Judea; this they did, sending it to the elders by Barnabas and Saul. (Acts 11:27-30)

> On the contrary, when they saw that I had been entrusted with the gospel for the uncircumcised, just as Peter had been entrusted with the gospel for the circumcised (for he who worked through Peter making him an apostle to the circumcised also worked through me in sending me to the gentiles), and when James and Cephas and John, who were acknowledged pillars, recognised the grace that had been given to me, they gave to Barnabas and me the right hand of fellowship, agreeing that we should go to the gentiles and they to the circumcised. They asked only one thing, that we remember the poor, which was actually what I was eager to do. (Gal 2:7-10)

It is mentioned again elsewhere.

To the Corinthians, he gives quite practical advice about the actual gathering of the donations.

> Now concerning the collection for the saints: you should follow the directions I gave to the churches of Galatia. On the first day of every week, each of you is to put aside and save whatever extra you earn, so that collections need not be taken when I come. And when I arrive, I will send any whom you approve with letters to take your gift to Jerusalem. If it seems advisable that I should go also, they will accompany me. (1 Cor 16:1-4)

To the Romans, he expressed his fear about returning to Jerusalem and what might await him there.

> At present, however, I am going to Jerusalem in a ministry to the saints; for Macedonia and Achaia have been pleased to share their resources with the poor among the saints at Jerusalem. They were pleased to do this, and indeed they owe it to them; for if the Gentiles have come to share in their spiritual blessings, they ought also to be of service to them in material things. So, when I have completed this, and have delivered to them what has been collected, I will set out by way of you to Spain; and I know that when I come to you, I will come in the fullness of the blessing of Christ. I appeal to you, brothers and sisters, by our Lord Jesus Christ and by the love of the Spirit, to join me in earnest prayer to God on my behalf, that I may be rescued from the unbelievers in Judea, and that my ministry to Jerusalem may be acceptable to the saints, so that by God's will I may come to you with joy and be refreshed in your company. (Rom 15:25-32)

Those fears were realised when Paul actually went there, because his presence there led to his arrest, to his journey to Rome, and conceivably to his death.

> When the governor motioned to him to speak, Paul replied: 'I cheerfully make my defense, knowing that for many years you have been a judge over this nation. As you can find out, it is not more than twelve days since I went up to worship in Jerusalem. They did not find me disputing with anyone in the temple or stirring up a crowd either in the synagogues or throughout the city. Neither can they prove to you the charge that they now bring against me. But this I admit to you, that according to the Way, which they call a sect, I worship the God of our ancestors, believing everything laid down according to the law or written in the prophets. I have a hope in God – a hope that they themselves also accept – that there will be a resurrection of both the righteous and the unrighteous. Therefore I do my best always to have a clear conscience toward God and all people. Now after some years I came to bring alms to my nation and to offer sacrifices. While I was doing this, they found me in the temple, completing the rite of purification, without any crowd or disturbance. But there were some Jews from Asia – they ought to be here before you to make an accusation, if they have anything against me. Or let these men here tell what crime they had found when I stood before the council, unless it was this one sentence that I called out while standing before them, "It is about the resurrection of the dead that I am on trial before you today."' (Acts 24:10-21)

the Way

The other place where Paul speaks of the collection at length is *2 Corinthians* 8-9. These chapters will be examined presently. But first all, a word about *2 Corinthians*.

EXERCISE 11:

a) What was the importance of the Jerusalem Collection for Paul? Write 5 lines.

b) What was Paul's general attitude to receiving money from communities? Write 5 lines.

UNIT FIVE
SECTION SIX

4. 2 CORINTHIANS

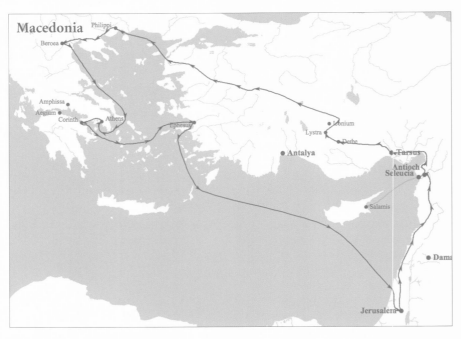

Fig. 14: *Paul's Second Missionary Journey*

As was seen earlier in this study, scholars have queried the integrity of the letters of Paul. It would seem clear that something happened when the letters were collected and it is at least possible that the present letters may contain multiple documents resulting in compilations. 2 *Corinthians* is a remarkable case in point, because it seems to show breaks and insertions. These are commonly noted in scholarly publications, though of course, there is little agreement about the resolution of these apparent tensions.

4.1 2 CORINTHIANS 2:13 AND 7:5

It looks as if the continuation of 2:13 should be 7.5.

> When I came to Troas to proclaim the good news of Christ, a door was opened for me in the Lord; but my mind could not rest because I did not find my brother Titus there. So I said farewell to them and went on to Macedonia. (2 Cor 2:12-13)

> For even when we came into Macedonia, our bodies had no rest, but we were afflicted in every way – disputes without and fears within. But God, who consoles the downcast, consoled us by the arrival of Titus, and not only by his coming, but also by the consolation with which he was consoled about you, as he told us of your longing, your mourning, your zeal for me, so that I rejoiced still more. (2 Cor 7:5-7)

4.2 2 CORINTHIANS 6:13 AND 7:2

It also looks as if 6:13 would be better served by going straight on to 7.2. In any case the intervening verses do not fit where they stand.

> In return – I speak as to children – open wide your hearts also. (2 Cor 6:13)

> Make room in your hearts for us; we have wronged no one, we have corrupted no one, we have taken advantage of no one. (2 Cor 7:2)

4.3   2 CORINTHIANS 6:14-7:1

The intervening verses (from 6:14 to 7:1) not only do not fit the context, the language seems somewhat unusual for Paul.

4.4   2 CORINTHIANS 8 AND 9

Many scholars hold that chapters 8 and 9 were originally two distinct letters, actually written to different audiences with a view to getting money from them: the Achaians and the Corinthians. Verse 9:1 sounds like a beginning rather than a moment of continuity of discussion.

> Now it is not necessary for me to write you about the ministry to the saints, for I know your eagerness, which is the subject of my boasting about you to the people of Macedonia, saying that Achaia has been ready since last year; and your zeal has stirred up most of them. (2 Cor 9:1-2)

If 8 comes before 9, then Paul has written rather fully about the ministry to the saints, yet then apparently says that it is not necessary to write!

4.5   2 CORINTHIANS 10-13

If, as some scholars hold, 2 *Corinthians* 1-7 can be read coherently as a document and if 2 *Corinthians* 8-9 can be read as a gesture of reconciliation, the bluntness and anger of what follows makes for a hard transition.

> I myself, Paul, appeal to you by the meekness and gentleness of Christ – I who am humble when face to face with you, but bold toward you when I am away! – I ask that when I am present I need not show boldness by daring to oppose those who think we are acting according to human standards. Indeed, we live as human beings, but we do not wage war according to human standards; for the weapons of our warfare are not merely human, but they have divine power to destroy strongholds. We destroy arguments and every proud obstacle raised up against the knowledge of God, and we take every thought captive to obey Christ. We are ready to punish every disobedience when your obedience is complete. (2 Cor 10:1-6)

So, all things considered, there are indeed problems with the integrity of 2 *Corinthians*. The focus in this particular unit will be on the two middle chapters, 8 and 9, which will be turned to presently.

EXERCISE 12:

a) Outline the evidence for or against the integrity of 2 Corinthians. Write 5 lines.

5.   2 CORINTHIANS 8-9

Hans Dieter Betz of the University of Chicago offers a reading of these two chapters which accepts that there are two distinct documents, each with its own epistolary and rhetorical structure.

The letter to the Corinthians			The letter to the Achaians		
Omit		**Letter opening**	**Omit**		**Letter opening**
1-24		Body of the letter	1-15		Body of the letter
	1-5	Introduction		1-2	Introduction
	6	Statement of facts		3-5a	Statement of facts
	7-9	Thesis		5bc	Thesis
	9-15	Proofs		6-14	Proofs
		9. Proof 1			6. Thesis
		10-12 Proof 2			7. Proof 1
		13-15 Proof 3			8. Proof 2
					9-11. Proof 3
					12. Proof 4
					13-14. Proof 5
	16-22	Commendation			
	23	Authorisation			
	24	Conclusion		15	Conclusion
Omit		Letter closing	Omit		Letter closing

This is a complex presentation, so a more simple one will now be offered.

When account is taken of the vocabulary used (delimitation) and the rhetorical layout of the two chapters, it is possible to see them as a unit of communication with its own overall structure which makes sense without extra hypotheses.

Rhetoric			**Verses**	**Topics**
Introduction	*Exordium*		8:1-6	Topic, history, people involved
Thesis	*Propositio*		8:7,(8)	Give to this project
Proofs	*Probationes*			
		Proof 1	8:9-15	Why donate?
		Proof 2	8:16-24	Honour and transparency
		Proof 3	9:1-5	Honour and freedom
		Proof 4	9:6-10	God rewards generosity
Conclusion	*Peroratio*		9:11-15	Thanksgiving to God

The usefulness of this pattern is that it respects two crucial issues in any appeal for money. The first issue is always, Why give at all? Paul responds to this in Proof 1 and Proof 4. Proof 1 proposes that those who give will be modelling themselves on Christ who made himself poor that we might become rich. In many ways this is a proof which must be convincing in a faith context. Proof 4 proposes that God rewards those who give and that God 'loves a cheerful giver'. Again this is something which is always true, and independent of the particular appeal. The technical term for these kinds of proofs, which are in some ways 'always true', is *questio infinita*. Infinita here means the proposal stands independently of all concrete, finite, circumstances.

questio infinita

The second issue is always: Why should someone respond to this proposal and give to these people? Behind this dimension stands the question of integrity and trustworthiness. Paul deals with the transparency of the collection in Proof 2 by naming the committee charged with carrying out the collection. Furthermore he underlines his own relative non-involvement by saying he hopes that the collection will be complete by the time he himself arrives in Corinth. While in some senses his honour was at stake in Proof 2, in Proof 3 it is the good name or honour of the Corinthians which is at stake. The technical term for this kind of practical consideration was *questio finita*. *Finita* here means that the proposal is concrete and finite, tied to these people and these circumstances.

questio finita

Fig. 15: *Telemachus, Nestor and Polycaste*

The handbooks of rhetoric taught that weak arguments should be bolstered, so to speak, by strong arguments. If, for example, you had three arguments and one was weaker than the others, it was recommended that the weak argument be placed in the middle, bolstered by the firmer arguments on either side. This careful gauging and placing of arguments is called 'Nestorian' after the commander Nestor in Homer. When fighting a battle with troops of variable quality, Nestor's practice was to put the strong ones at the front and the back and put the weaker ones in the middle. It is in the nature of arguments that the *questio infinita*, because it is always true, is strong, while the *questio finita*, because it is true only in these circumstances, is weak. Therefore, Paul makes use of the Nestorian layout here, placing the weaker, practical arguments in the centre, bolstered on the outside by the stronger, theoretical arguments.

Nestorian placement

Type of argument		Verses	Contents
Questio infinita		8:8-15 **A**	Give generously; the example of Christ; the principle of equality; in time of need, your want will be reward; scripture citation to conclude.
	Questio finita	8:16-24 **B**	Paul's integrity and honour; transparency of administration; the churches as witnesses.
	Questio finita	9:1-5 **B¹**	Paul's good name; reputation and honour of the Corinthians; Paul's detachment from the practical collection of the money.
Questio infinita		9:6-10 **A¹**	Give generously; it is part of your relationship with God; God will reward you; scripture citations to conclude.

The presentation falls into to pattern ABB¹A¹ which makes for a very clear presentation. Each stage of the rhetorical structure will now be examined briefly, starting with the introduction, and concluding with a comparison of the conclusion and the introduction.

UNIT FIVE
SECTION SIX

5.1   INTRODUCTION

¹We want you to know, brothers and sisters, about the grace of God that has been granted to the churches of Macedonia; ²for during a severe ordeal of affliction, their abundant joy and their extreme poverty have overflowed in a wealth of generosity on their part. ³For, as I can testify, they voluntarily gave according to their means, and even beyond their means, ⁴begging us earnestly for the privilege of sharing in this ministry to the saints – ⁵and this, not merely as we expected; they gave themselves first to the Lord and, by the will of God, to us, ⁶so that we might urge Titus that, as he had already made a beginning, so he should also complete this generous undertaking among you. (2 Cor 8:1-6)

The function of the introduction was to get people's attention, good will and receptivity. Attention is achieved here by praising the church of Macedonia. The Achaians would surely begin to make comparisons with themselves. Receptivity is guaranteed by the sequence of requests: the Macedonians gave themselves to the Lord and then to Paul, and Paul then urged Titus. This means that the proposal, in some sense, comes not directly from Paul but from God, through the Macedonians! In faith discourse, God's initiative must always be listened to. Finally, he reminds them that a beginning had already been made. There is a risk in such untrammelled praise of the Macedonians, impoverished as they were. Was Paul asking the Achaians to impoverish themselves?

5.2   THESIS

⁷Now as you excel in everything – in faith, in speech, in knowledge, in utmost eagerness, and in our love for you – so we want you to excel also in this generous undertaking. ⁸I do not say this as a command, but I am testing the genuineness of your love against the earnestness of others. (2 Cor 8:7-8)

Verse 7 here is the thesis. It moves through three moments.

- The first moment is praise: 'you excel in everything'. Praise is always acceptable and encouraging.

- The second moment is a subtle one. Paul lists the things in which the Corinthians excel – faith, speech, knowledge, eagerness – the very things for which he reproves them in 1 *Corinthians*. Then he adds an unexpected element, 'and in our love for you'. One would have anticipated 'in your love for us', which would always be something excellent. However, expressed the other way around – our love for you – it is a reminder that they are, so to speak, net beneficiaries in their relationship with Paul. It is a way of marking with sensitivity, yet unmistakably, their indebtedness to him.

- The third moment is a straight appeal to continue in excellence: 'so we want you to excel also in this generous undertaking'.

Verse 8 is an attempt to take the harm out of the recall of their indebtedness to Paul. It is not a command. On the contrary, it is a freely-given opportunity to excel. Nevertheless, the message is entirely clear.

5.3   PROOF 1

⁹For you know the generous act of our Lord Jesus Christ, that though he was rich, yet for your sakes he became poor, so that by his poverty you might become rich. ¹⁰And in this matter I am giving my advice: it is appropriate for you who began last year not only to do something but even to desire to do something – ¹¹now finish doing it, so that your eagerness may be matched by completing it according to your means. ¹²For if the eagerness is there, the gift is acceptable according to what one has – not according to what one does not have. ¹³I do not mean that there should be relief for others and pressure on you, but it is a question of a fair balance between ¹⁴your present abundance and their need, so that their abundance may be for your need, in order that there may be a fair balance. ¹⁵As it is written, 'The one who had much did not have too much, and the one who had little did not have too little.' (2 Cor 8:9-15)

The first general argument (*questio infinita*) begins with the most powerful persuasion in a faith context, the example of Christ himself in verse 9. There is a risk here because no one makes himself voluntarily poor, so Paul has to moderate the implications of the example. Thus in verses 10-14, he notes that he is not asking them to make themselves radically poor, but rather to give in proportion to what they actually have. At some time in the future, perhaps the recipients will be able to return to the favour. The quotation from Scripture is an adjusted reference to Exodus 16:8.

But when they measured it with an omer, those who gathered much had nothing over, and those who gathered little had no shortage; they gathered as much as each of them needed. (Exod 16:18)

As can be seen, Paul has adjusted the citation to make it more balanced, in order to reflect the balance he had just spoken about.

5.4   PROOF 2

¹⁶But thanks be to God who put in the heart of Titus the same eagerness for you that I myself have. ¹⁷For he not only accepted our appeal, but since he is more eager than ever, he is going to you of his own accord. ¹⁸With him we are sending the brother who is famous among all the churches for his proclaiming the good news; ¹⁹and not only that, but he has also been appointed by the churches to travel with us while we are administering this generous undertaking for the glory of the Lord himself and to show our goodwill. ²⁰We intend that no one should blame us about this generous gift that we are administering, ²¹for we intend to do what is right not only in the Lord's sight but also in the sight of others. ²²And with them we are sending our brother whom we have often tested and found eager in many matters, but who is now more eager than ever because of his great confidence in you. ²³As for Titus, he is my partner and co-worker in your service; as for our brothers, they are messengers of the churches, the glory of Christ. ²⁴Therefore openly before the churches, show them the proof of your love and of our reason for boasting about you. (2 Cor 8:16-24)

Fig. 16: *Titus*

Notice the team being presented: Titus (at God's inspiration), a brother known to the churches, and yet another brother, whose integrity is known. Three people would oversee the collection, and Paul himself would not put a hand on the money. It may seem a bit mean, but it looks as if some in Corinth were wondering if the apostle was putting his hand in the till. Paul deftly extricates himself from that possible construction. In a sense, that is at a political level. At the theological level, Paul emphasised God's guidance in this affair: God put it into the heart of Titus; and it was for the glory of the Lord. It is possible that the last part of verse 23 should read as an exclamation, 'Christ's (be) the glory', which would be a third theological dimension.

The last verse is both an end and a beginning. It ends this part of the persuasion which began with the wish 'so we want you to excel also in this generous undertaking' (2 Cor 8:7). It also leads to the next paragraph, when Paul uses his own absence to put pressure on the Corinthians.

5.5   PROOF 3

[1]Now it is not necessary for me to write you about the ministry to the saints, [2]for I know your eagerness, which is the subject of my boasting about you to the people of Macedonia, saying that Achaia has been ready since last year; and your zeal has stirred up most of them. [3]But I am sending the brothers in order that our boasting about you may not prove to have been empty in this case, so that you may be ready, as I said you would be; [4]otherwise, if some Macedonians come with me and find that you are not ready, we would be humiliated – to say nothing of you – in this undertaking. [5]So I thought it necessary to urge the brothers to go on ahead to you, and arrange in advance for this bountiful gift that you have promised, so that it may be ready as a voluntary gift and not as an extortion. (2 Cor 9:1-5)

In this passage, Paul picks up on the implied comparison between the Macedonians and the Corinthians and makes it explicit. More than that, he himself is not coming, which might be perceived as offensive. Paul, however, turns it into an occasion of freedom – without the pressure of his presence, they can feel free to give what they should give. However, if they give nothing or even very little he will be humiliated, and so he adds, 'to say nothing of you'! It is a sharp moment but made more acceptable by the idea that he was not trying to force them but to leave them free to give as they can.

5.6   PROOF 4

[6]The point is this: the one who sows sparingly will also reap sparingly, and the one who sows bountifully will also reap bountifully. [7]Each of you must give as you have made up your mind, not reluctantly or under compulsion, for God loves a cheerful giver. [8]And God is able to provide you with every blessing in abundance, so that by always having enough of everything, you may share abundantly in every good work. [9]As it is written,

> 'He scatters abroad, he gives to the poor;
>
> his righteousness endures forever.'

[10]He who supplies seed to the sower and bread for food will supply and multiply your seed for sowing and increase the harvest of your righteousness. (2 Cor 9:6-10)

Here Paul is on more solid ground with the return to the *questio infinita*. God's reward for generosity is, as noted above, always true in a faith context. Again, the reader will notice the balanced sentences which open this proof. In Greek, it is even more striking, with the words 'sparingly' and 'bountifully' immediately repeated: 'The one who sows sparingly, sparingly will also reap, and the one who sows bountifully, bountifully will also reap.' Once more, a citation caps the persuasion and is immediately amplified in a comment. The word righteousness anticipates a wider use of early catechetical vocabulary in the conclusion which follows.

EXERCISE 13:

a) *Describe either Proof 1 or Proof 4. Write 5 lines.*

b) *Describe either Proof 2 or Proof 3. Write 5 lines.*

5.7 CONCLUSION

[11]You will be enriched in every way for your great generosity, which will produce thanksgiving to God through us; [12]for the rendering of this ministry not only supplies the needs of the saints but also overflows with many thanksgivings to God. [13]Through the testing of this ministry you glorify God by your obedience to the confession of the gospel of Christ and by the generosity of your sharing with them and with all others, [14]while they long for you and pray for you because of the surpassing grace of God that he has given you. [15]Thanks be to God for his indescribable gift! (2 Cor 9:11-15)

Introduction	Conclusion
[8:1]We want you to know, brothers and sisters, about the **grace** of God that has been granted to the churches of Macedonia; [2]for during a severe ordeal of affliction, their abundant joy and their extreme poverty have overflowed in a **wealth of generosity** on their part. [3]For, as I can testify, they voluntarily gave according to their means, and even beyond their means, [4]begging us earnestly for the privilege of **sharing** in this **ministry** to the **saints** – [5]and this, not merely as we expected; they gave themselves first to the Lord and, by the **will** of God, to us, [6]so that we might urge Titus that, as he had already made a beginning, so he should also complete this **generous undertaking** among you.	[9:11]You will be **enriched** in every way for your great **generosity**, which will produce *thanksgiving* to God through us; [12]for the rendering of this **ministry** not only supplies the needs of the **saints** but also overflows with many *thanksgivings* to God. [13]Through the testing of this **ministry** you glorify God by your **obedience** to the confession of the gospel of Christ and by the **generosity** of your **sharing** with them and with all others, [14]while they long for you and pray for you because of the surpassing **grace** of God that he has given you. [15]***Thanks*** be to God for his indescribable **gift**!

In contrast to Betz, others think this is the final conclusion to the whole persuasion. There are three reasons for this:

a) There is a frame. 'Thanksgiving to God' in verse 11 is echoed in 'Thanks to God' in verse 15.

b) The vocabulary becomes enriched with the language of the early Christian proclamation, the *kerygma* (the Greeks terms are transliterated below to give the proper flavour):

[11]You will be enriched in every way for your great generosity, which will produce thanksgiving (*eucharistia*) to God through us; [12]for the rendering (*diakonia*) of this ministry (*leitourgia*) not only supplies the needs of the saints (*hagioi*) but also overflows with many thanksgivings (*eucharistia*) to God. [13]Through the testing of this ministry (*diakonia*) you glorify God by your obedience to the confession (*homologia*) of the gospel (*euangelion*) of Christ and by the generosity of your sharing (*koinonia*) with them and with all others, [14]while they long for you and pray for you because of the surpassing grace (*charis*) of God that he has given you. [15]Thanks (*charis*) be to God for his indescribable gift (*dorea*)! (2 Cor 9:11-15)

eucharistia
diakonia
leitourgia
hagioi
eucharistia
diakonia
homologia
euangelion
koinonia
charis
dorea

The evocation of such powerful religious language would have a tremendous influence on believers. Paul, in effect, was saying that they will be putting into practice their Christian identity if they take part in his project. That is a large claim, but Paul does not shrink from it.

c)   As expected, there is a correspondence between the introduction and the conclusion, a regular feature in Paul.

Thus, Paul draws his argument to a close by evoking the opening challenge.

Fig. 17: *The Acrocorinth*

CONCLUSIONS TO UNIT FIVE

I   PAUL'S RHETORIC

A number of conclusions may be drawn from this analysis.

a)   It shows Paul, once more, as an adept user of the techniques of persuasion available in the culture.

b)   It shows Paul as a practical theologian. He has a project which has a theological basis: the mutual belonging of the church of the circumcision and the church of the gentiles. There are two sides to the collection. It is first of all something practical; but it is also a symbol, an effective sign of indebtedness of the gentiles to the Jews. Paul brings a great deal of theology to bear: God, who loves a cheerful giver; Christ, who made himself poor that we might become rich; the realisation of Christian identity as found in the compendium of catechetical vocabulary in the conclusion.

c)   Finally, it shows Paul as the master organiser. In the interests of transparency, the committee is made up of people of known integrity from different sides. In the interests of his own honour, Paul detaches himself both by space and by time. He will not be there when the collection is made and he hopes it will be done before he arrives. This puts tremendous pressure on the Corinthians who will have to prove their mettle in the face of outsiders of some standing. The risk of sending in others is turned around, however, by Paul and converted into an opportunity for freedom! The whole communication is quite masterful.

2. LEARNING OUTCOMES ASSESSED

By the end of this unit, in addition to the learning outcomes listed at the start of the unit, students should:

a) have a grasp of the setting of the Pauline correspondence, with special attention to:

  i. the history and archaeology of Corinth, and

  ii. the membership of the Corinthian churches.

b) be able to explain the occasion and structure of 1 *Corinthians*;

c) understand Paul's theology of the cross (1 Cor 1-4);

d) analyse the practice of the Lord's Supper (1 Cor 11);

e) locate 1 *Corinthians* 13 within the discussion of the spiritual gifts (1 Cor 12-14);

f) appreciate the theology and rhetoric of 1 *Corinthians* 15;

g) account for the persuasive structure of 2 *Corinthians* 8-9; and

h) be aware of the theology behind the Jerusalem collection.

THE LETTER TO THE PHILIPPIANS

INTRODUCTION TO UNIT SIX

Fig. 18: *Saint Paul*

I. INTRODUCTION

As often noted, Paul is the earliest Christian writer whose documents have survived. By the time the gospels were written, Paul was already dead, but his letters were circulating widely. It seems astonishing, therefore, that they are so rich in content. The question asked of Jesus could also have been asked of Paul: 'Where did this man get all this? What is this wisdom that has been given to him?' (Mk 6:2). Paul had an immense amount of background knowledge of the Bible (the Hebrew Bible, that is), and had always been a person of faith. The religious experience of his so-called conversion was clearly the great turning point of his life. He had further religious experiences, such as the one cautiously recounted in 2 *Corinthians* 12. Now and again in his writings he mentioned something he had received 'as a word from the Lord', meaning an inspired discernment, under the power of the Holy Spirit (1 Thess 4:15; 1 Cor 14:37; 2 Cor 12:9). The richness of his writings was also the fruit of his familiarity with the Christian tradition. This started even before his conversion. It is unthinkable that Paul persecuted Christians without having had some knowledge of what they were proclaiming. That proclamation would have included the acclamations 'Amen',

'Abba Father', 'Maranatha', 'Jesus is the Christ' and 'Jesus is Lord', and the incipiently creedal elements such as 'Jesus is risen from the dead'.

Once Paul had become convinced of Jesus' resurrection, a rich range of traditions was at his disposal. Traditional elements may also be noticed in his recounting of the Lord's Supper (1 Cor 11:23ff and 1 Cor 15:1-3). There is a mention, for example, of Christian hymns in 1 *Corinthians* 14:26. As well as the Lord's Supper, Paul was aware of baptism (Rom 6:1ff.). Christian hymns can be detected (for example, in *Philippians* 2:6-11, 1 *Corinthians* 13 and *Romans* 11:33-36). This unit will be devoted primarily to a reading of the hymn in *Philippians*.

2.   LEARNING OUTCOMES

By the end of this unit, students should fully grasp:

a)   the problem of the chronology of *Philippians*;

b)   the setting of the letter in the life of Paul; and

c)   the hymn in *Philippians* 2:6-11.

SECTION ONE:
GEOGRAPHY AND RHETORIC

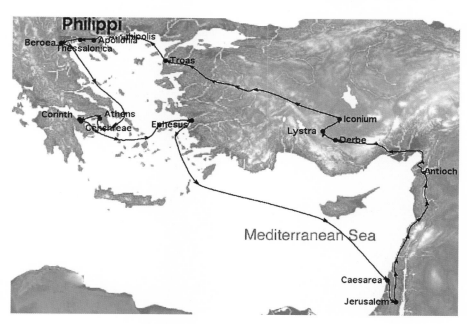

Fig. 19: *Paul's Second Missionary Journey*

I.   BACKGROUND

Philippi was Paul's first community in Europe, founded on his second missionary journey. This can be known from 1 *Thessalonians* and 2 *Corinthians*, as can his attachment to the Philippians and they to him. The dating of the letter itself is disputed. Conceivably, it could have been written from Rome, Caesarea or Ephesus.

Traditionally, the letter was thought to have been written from Rome, just before Paul's own martyrdom. This would make the *Letter to the Philippians* his last letter, and would document the apostle's state of mind right up to the end, perhaps 64 ce. The chief geographical evidence is found in his reference to the praetorium (1:13) and to the household of Caesar (4:22). But such details could fit other cities as well. Caesarea is also mentioned as a possibility. However the letter presupposes Paul's visiting back and forth, which might have been difficult with such a great distance (2:19-30; 4:16-18). A more recent proposal is the obvious Ephesus, about a week's distance from Philippi. This would imply a date somewhere in the mid 50s.

From the letter itself, it is possible to reconstruct the following sequence:

a)   the Philippians learn of Paul's imprisonment;

b)   they send Epaphroditus with a gift for Paul;

c)   Epaphroditus falls seriously ill on his way to Paul and nearly dies;

d)   The Philippians learn of Epaphroditus' illness and become concerned;

e)   Epaphroditus recovers, completes his journey to Paul, and delivers the gift;

f)   Epaphroditus learns of the Philippians' anxiety for him and becomes distressed; and

g)   Paul sends Epaphroditus back to Philippi with a letter in which he commends Epaphroditus, he thanks the Philippians for their gift, warns them about false teachers, and informs them about his own circumstances and plans.

2.   A LETTER AND A SPEECH

Verses	Letter	Speech[11]	Topic
1:1-2	Superscript		Greeting
1:3-11	Thanksgiving	Introduction	
1:12-26	Body	Statement of Facts	
1:27-30		Thesis	
2:1-3:19		Proof	
3:20-4:20		Conclusion	
4:21-23	Postscript		Greeting

The hymn which will now be analysed is found in the first development of the proof, that is, within 2:1-18. The context is the quality of relationships within the community, and the model and example of Christ.

3.   PHILIPPIANS 2:6-11

[5]Let the same mind be in you that was in Christ Jesus,
        [6]who, though he was in the form of God,
                did not regard equality with God
                as something to be exploited,
        [7]but emptied himself,
                taking the form of a slave,
                being born in human likeness.
And being found in human form,
        [8]he humbled himself
                and became obedient to the point of death –
                even death on a cross.

        [9]Therefore God also highly exalted him
                and gave him the name
                that is above every name,
        [10]so that at the name of Jesus
                every knee should bend,
                in heaven and on earth and under the earth,
        [11]and every tongue should confess
                that Jesus Christ is Lord,

---

11.   Hayden, C.: *Pauline Rhetoric in the Service of the Heavenly Politeuma*, unpublished doctoral thesis, Milltown Institute (2008).

3.1   *GENRE*

There are two categories or *genres* of hymns in the New Testament. The first category includes those that are doctrinal, didactic or liturgical in scope.

- Some examples of this first category can be found in Ephesians 5:14; 1 Timothy 3:16 and 6:15-16; 2 Timothy 2:11-13; Titus 3:4-7; *Philippians* 2:6-11; and Revelation 22:17.

- In the second category are those that are doxological in content. These are all found in the *Book of Revelation* (1:4-8; 4:8; 4:11; 5:9-10; 5:12; 11:15; 11:17-18; and 15:3-4).

3.2   BACKGROUND

Scholars have wondered about the religious and cultural background to this hymn, and a variety of suggestions is offered:

a)   The 'primal man' myth;

b)   The *Genesis* story of Adam as well as later Jewish speculation about two Adams;

c)   The Deutero-Isaianic figure of the Suffering Servant; and

d)   The figure of divine Wisdom in hellenistic Judaism.

It is very likely that a number of potential references should be kept in mind, including Adam, the Suffering Servant and Wisdom speculation.

3.3   POETRY

Many proposals have been made to analyse the hymn in strophes and to see if Pauline editorial retouches can be detected. Here, the two main proposals are presented.

Proposal 1

A hymn in six strophes of three lines each, with Paul's editorial additions in italics:

A   ⁶who, though he was in the form of God,
          did not regard equality with God
          as something to be exploited,

B   ⁷but emptied himself,
          taking the form of a slave,
          being born in human likeness.

C   And being found in human form,
          ⁸he humbled himself
          and became obedient to the point of death –
          even death on a cross.

D   ⁹Therefore God also highly exalted him
          and gave him the name
          that is above every name,

E   ¹⁰so that at the name of Jesus
          every knee should bend,
          in heaven and on earth and under the earth,

F   ¹¹and every tongue should confess
          that Jesus Christ is Lord,
          to the glory of God the Father.

Proposal II

A hymn of three strophes of four lines each, with Paul's editorial additions in italics:

A ⁶who, though he was in the form of God,
did not regard equality with God
as something to be exploited, ⁷but emptied himself,
taking the form of a slave,

B being born in human likeness.
And being found in human form,
⁸he humbled himself
and became obedient to the point of death –
even death on a cross.

C ⁹Therefore God also highly exalted him
and gave him the name that is above every name,
¹⁰so that at the name of Jesus every knee should bend,
in heaven and on earth and under the earth,
¹¹and every tongue should confess that Jesus Christ is Lord,
to the glory of God the Father.

The discussion of this hymn has given rise to a huge number of studies. However, it is sufficient here to notice that the text really is a hymn and can be analysed as such.

3.4 COMMENT

The christology of the hymn resembles material found elsewhere in the New Testament.

> Paul an apostle – sent neither by human commission nor from human authorities, but through Jesus Christ and God the Father, who raised him from the dead – and all the members of God's family who are with me, To the churches of Galatia: Grace to you and peace from God our Father and the Lord Jesus Christ, who gave himself for our sins to set us free from the present evil age, according to the will of our God and Father, to whom be the glory forever and ever. Amen. (Gal 1:1-5)

> Now in subjecting all things to them, God left nothing outside their control. As it is, we do not yet see everything in subjection to them, but we do see Jesus, who for a little while was made lower than the angels, now crowned with glory and honour because of the suffering of death, so that by the grace of God he might taste death for everyone. (Heb 2:8-9)

The introduction 'stitches' the hymn into the ethical persuasion: 'Let the same mind be in you that was in Christ Jesus' (Phil 2:5). 'Mind' in Greek is really the verb 'to think'. A good parallel in Paul would be *Romans 12:3*:

> ⁶who, though he was in the form of God,
> did not regard equality with God
> as something to be exploited,

Form (Greek: *morphé*) is difficult to translate. It was used in classical and Hellenistic Greek with a wide range of meanings (stature, form, condition, feature, external appearance, reproduction). *Morphé* is used relatively little in the Bible. 'Exploited' is also a difficult word: it may mean not only 'to grasp something forcefully which one does not have' but also 'to retain by force what one possesses'.

> [7]but emptied himself,
>> taking the form of a slave,
>> being born in human likeness.
> And being found in human form,

'Emptied' in relation to the cross comes up in 1 *Corinthians* 1:17. It is a striking image, intimating that Jesus had 'set aside' his pre-existent status. Notice the repetition of the form (Greek: *morphé*) of a slave.

> [8]he humbled himself
> and became obedient to the point of death –
> even death on a cross.

'Humility' is found repeatedly in the teaching of Jesus (Mt 18:4;23:12; Lk 3:5;14:11;18:14). 'Obedience unto death' is found elsewhere in the New Testament (Heb 2:10-18). Verse 8c 'death on a cross' could be an addition made by Paul reflecting his repeated theological emphasis on the cross (Phil 1:29, 3:10,18 and 1 Cor 1:23; 2:2).

> [9]Therefore God also highly exalted him
>> and gave him the name
>> that is above every name,

The simple form of 'exalted' is found in *John* and *Luke* to refer to the resurrection (Jn 3:14; 8:28; 12:32, 34; Acts 2:33; 5:31). The complex form is found only here in the New Testament and in the LXX only once: 'For you, O LORD, are most high over all the earth; you are exalted far above all gods.' (LXX Ps 96:9)

> [10]so that at the name of Jesus
>> every knee should bend,
>> in heaven and on earth and under the earth,

There is a suggestion that this verse may be a liturgical instruction, advising worshippers of the required bodily gesture at this point,

> [11]and every tongue should confess
>> that Jesus Christ is Lord,
>> to the glory of God the Father.

'Confess' (Greek: *homologeó*) is a foundational Christian word, both as a verb and as a noun (Mt 7:23; 10:32; 14:7; Lk 12:8; Jn 1:20; 9:22; 12:42; Acts 7:17; 23:8; 24:14, etc.). 'Jesus is Lord' is a basic affirmation found clearly in Paul:

> Because if you confess with your lips that Jesus is Lord and believe in your heart that God raised him from the dead, you will be saved. (Rom 10:9)

And:

> Therefore I want you to understand that no one speaking by the Spirit of God ever says 'Let Jesus be cursed!' and no one can say 'Jesus is Lord' except by the Holy Spirit. (1 Cor 12:3)

EXERCISE 1:

a) What is the place of Philippians in the writings of Paul? Write 5 lines.

b) Describe the christological hymn in Philippians and outlined its understanding of Christ? Write 10 lines.

UNIT SIX CONCLUSIONS

Fig. 20: *Ancient shrines from the city of Philippi*

1. THE PRE-EXISTENCE OF CHRIST

The hymn in *Philippians* provides a window on the early Christian world of worship and faith, a world which in some ways pre-dates the surviving documents of Paul himself. It is a text which underlines both the pre-existence of Christ and the humanity of Jesus. Paul's use of the hymn in *Philippians* is also interesting: he wanted to promote communion, mutual acceptance and tolerance. His highest example and motivation is Jesus himself, and this example was adopted by using a hymn already familiar to the Church. It has not lost its force for the present generation of Christians.

2. LEARNING OUTCOMES ASSESSED

By the end of this unit, in addition to the learning outcomes listed at the start of the unit, students should be able to:

a)   discuss the problem of the chronology of *Philippians*;

b)   locate the letter in the life and teaching of Paul; and

c)   be able to discuss the various issues which arise out of the hymn in *Philippians* 2:6-11.

PROGRAMME
THEOLOGY FOR TODAY

MODULE
THE PAULINE WRITINGS

UNIT SEVEN
THE LETTER TO THE ROMANS

INTRODUCTION TO UNIT SEVEN

Fig. 21: Roman Ghetto

1. INTRODUCTION

Paul's *Letter to the Romans* is one of the great Christian documents – great in itself and great in its continued resonance down the centuries. It is a long letter, and one often has the feeling that it is more a treatise that a letter. Nevertheless, it can be located within the context on the Roman Christian churches and that context helps a great deal in understanding the chief arguments and the letter's structure.

2. CONTENT OF THE UNIT

This unit investigates the history of the Jewish community in Rome and the history of the Christian communities in Rome. It examines the purpose and structure of the *Letter to the Romans*, placing a special emphasis on the theological content of the letter.

3. LEARNING OUTCOMES

At the end of this unit, students should know:

a)   how Christianity arrived in Rome;

b)   the history of the Christian movement in Rome;

c)   why Paul wrote to the Roman communities; and

d)   the overall argument and lay-out of the letter;

e)   *Romans* 1: 16-4 :25: all in need before God;

f)   *Romans* 5-8: the gift in Christ;

g)   *Romans* 9-11: the relationship of Jews and Christians;

h)   *Romans* 12:1-15:6: the theology of tolerance;

i)   *Romans* 1:8-16 and 15:7-33: the links between the *exordium* and the *peroratio*; and

j)   *Romans* 1:1-7 and 16:1-27: the functions of the introduction and the conclusion.

SECTION ONE:
THE CONTEXT OF THE LETTER

I.   INTRODUCTION

 ## Task

a) Students should read the letter right through. It is not an easy read in all its parts, but registering one's own feeling for the letter is an important step in appreciating the document, even if it raises more questions than it answers.

Although the *Letter to the Romans* feels more like a theological treatise, it nevertheless is a real letter written to address a particular situation in the Roman churches. This section will look at four questions:

a)   What was Rome like at the period?

b)   Who were the Roman Christians?

c)   What was their history?

d)   What sources are available for these investigations?

2.   JEWS IN ROME

Rome was an immensely large city for the period, with approximately one million inhabitants. That very size made the city exceptional; at this point in history the vast majority of people still lived on the land. Even an important city like Corinth had only somewhere between eighty and a hundred thousand inhabitants. So, Rome at the time would have seemed extraordinary. If one considers only one practical matter, then the size of the problem becomes apparent: How did the city authorities supply such a huge population with water? But Rome was not impressive only for its size. It lay at the heart of an empire approaching its zenith, and the city was famous for its shrines and monuments, many of which still stand today.

Rome was an immensely multicultural place and, among other nationalities, it attracted Jews. It is not known just how many Jews lived there at the time but somewhere between one hundred and two hundred thousand may not be widely

Jewish tomb inscriptions
Jewish catacombs
synagogue

off the mark. It is very probable that these were originally drawn there by the potential for trade. Their traces can still be seen today in the many Jewish tomb inscriptions, Jewish catacombs, and the wonderful synagogue at Ostia Antica.

Fig. 22: *Remains of the Synagogue at Ostia*

The names of other synagogues have also survived, and these latter are extremely interesting because they show a high degree of inculturation, even in a hostile pagan environment.

Augustenses, Agrippenses, Herodienses, Volumnenses, Campenses, Siburenses, Calcarenses, Elea, Tripolitani, Sekenoi, Arca of Lebanon, Hebraei and Vernaculi

Some of the names denote origin, others refer to areas of the city and others again express devotion to the imperial and other powerful families, such as Augustenses, Agrippenses and Herodienses.

There is a dispute among scholars as to exactly where the Jews were located in the city. They were probably in more than one location. In the middle of the first century ce they had enough presence in the port district of ancient Rome, Ostia, to build a synagogue. The synagogue at Ostia, slightly difficult to access, is remarkable for being the earliest synagogue building in Europe which still has material remains. As it stands today (as a somewhat restored ruin), it reflects more its condition in the fourth century, just before the port of Ostia silted up and become unusable. It remains only a possibility, but an intriguing one nevertheless, that Paul could have visited this early synagogue during his time in Rome.

god-fearers

These god-fearing people would have formed the natural target audience for a preacher like Paul, who was offering the next stage of the same faith in God to gentiles, but explicitly without the ritual dimensions of the Law.

However, it must be noted that while Jews certainly lived in the city itself, no further Jewish buildings have survived. It may well be that just like its sister religion, Judaism was served by 'house synagogues'. It is also highly probable that, as elsewhere in the empire, the Jewish places of worship attracted also the 'god-fearers'. The god-fearers were gentiles convinced of monotheism who were attracted to the ethical ideals of Judaism, but who at the same time did not want to become Jews, for a whole variety of reasons. In any case, with the exception of the Pharisees, Judaism was not especially mission-oriented. These people would have formed the natural target audience for a preacher like Paul, who was offering the next stage of the same faith in God to the gentiles, but explicitly without the ritual dimensions of the Law. The question of how much of the Law ought to be observed by Christians became important for the Roman churches. Finally, while no one knows exactly how Christianity arrived in Rome, the probability is that it arrived through Jewish traders and grew slowly from these. In any case, by the time Paul wrote to them, they were a large enough group to have had a major and divisive row among themselves.

3. THE CHRISTIAN COMMUNITIES IN ROME

It is not easy to piece together the history of the Christian movement in Rome. However, there are traces of information in Roman historians of the period which can help. These involve two Roman emperors, Claudius (10 bce-54 ce) and his successor Nero (37-68 ce).

3.1 CLAUDIUS

Claudius became emperor in 41 ce. His accession was irregular. Having been found hiding in the palace behind a curtain, he was dragged off by the praetorians and proclaimed emperor. His niece Agrippina, who was also his fourth wife, had him poisoned in 54. His attitude to the Jews was, in general, enlightened, because Josephus reports that he issued an edict guaranteeing Jews throughout the empire the right to practise their religion 'without let or hindrance'.[12] Nevertheless, there is a report in Suentonius' *The Lives of the Twelve Caesars* which mentions an expulsion of Jews from Rome.

> Since the Jews constantly made disturbances at the instigation of Chrestus, [Claudius] expelled them from Rome.
> (Suetonius: *Lives, Claudius*, 25.4)

Claudius' expulsion of Jews from Rome is apparently confirmed by *Acts*:

> There he found a Jew named Aquila, a native of Pontus, who had recently come from Italy with his wife Priscilla, because Claudius had ordered all Jews to leave Rome. (Acts 18:2)

The phrase 'at the instigation of Chrestus' has given rise to much pondering. It is very likely that the Christian movement arrived in Rome among Jewish traders. At this early stage, Christianity would still have been seen as a movement within Judaism. As far as is known, Jews probably met in house synagogues. At some point in the time of Claudius, there was sufficient disagreement among those house synagogues for the dispute to come to the attention of the authorities. Roman city rulers were always anxious about civil disturbances and in this case they acted swiftly. To modern historians, it seems unlikely that all the Jews in Rome were expelled. To have rounded them all up and sent them away would have been excessive and unnecessary. As an excessive gesture it would have caused considerable economic disruption. As an unnecessary gesture, it would have given rise to great resentment. In reality, it would have been sufficient to expel those Jews causing the disturbance, that is, Jews convinced that Jesus was the Messiah. These would naturally have included Aquila and Priscilla (Prisca in the letters of Paul).

Although Chrestus has been mentioned, it is worth noting that the authorities and the historians did not distinguish between Jews and Christians at this stage.

3.2 NERO

Nero was originally named Domitius Ahenobarbus, was adopted by his step-father Claudius, and changed his name at the age of twelve to Nero Claudius Caesar Germanicus. It was precisely to ensure Nero's succession that Agrippina did away with Claudius, and accordingly Nero became emperor in 54 ce. Nero was the first emperor to persecute Christians actively.

Fig. 23: *Claudius*

Fig. 24: *Nero*

---

12. Josephus: *Ant* 19.290.

However, Nero failed to respond quickly enough to other military crises and was eventually abandoned by the praetorians and the Senate. He took refuge in the villa of his ex-slave Paon, and there he committed suicide, reportedly lamenting 'What an artist dies with me'.

Again, in his *Lives of the Caesars*,[13] Suetonius mentions the Christians as a 'class of men given to a new and mischievous superstition'. It is interesting to note that he calls the religion a new superstition and seems not to confuse it, as the earlier citation had done, with Judaism. This distinction is even clearer in the *Chronicle* of Sulpicius Severus.[14] Nero had been blamed for the fire in Rome and tried to deflect blame by punishing the Christians who by now had become a very large group. Finally, Tacitus wrote:

> But all human efforts, all the lavish gifts of the emperor, and the propitiations of the gods did not banish the sinister belief that the conflagration was the result of an order. Consequently, to get rid of the report, Nero fastened the guilt and inflicted the most exquisite tortures on a class hated for their abominations, called Christians by the populace.
>
> Christus, from whom the name had its origin, suffered the extreme penalty during the reign of Tiberius at the hands of one of our procurators, Pontius Pilatus, and a most mischievous superstition thus checked for the moment, again broke out not only in Judaea, the first source of the evil, but even in Rome, where all things hideous and shameful from every part of the world find their centre and become popular.
>
> (Tacitus: *Annals*, 15.44)

In the reign of Nero, the Roman authorities and writers were able to clearly distinguish Christians from Jews. How did it happen that they became, at least in Roman official eyes, separate and distinct? To explain this, scholars propose the following hypothesis.

At the start, Christians were Jews, and in that sense indistinguishable as a religion. They did of course attract gentiles, perhaps from that natural pool of potential converts, the god-fearers. As noted elsewhere, these were gentiles attracted to Judaism by its antiquity, monotheism and morality, but who did not wish to become Jews as such. This hesitation is understandable. Circumcision was not regarded as an embellishment, and the dietary laws made social intercourse very difficult. Within the Christian movement, however, there were no such requirements, and they could become full members without difficulty. It can be imagined, however, that in the early stages, such gentile god-fearers were relatively few in number.

Circumcision was not regarded as an embellishment, and the dietary laws made social intercourse very difficult.

Claudius did eventually expel the trouble-makers of the house synagogues, mostly, that is Jews. This would have had an immediate effect on the Christian movement. Hitherto, the Christians had been closely attached to the Jewish matrix, and it is more than likely that Jewish members continued their usual ritual practices. However, once the Christian Jews were removed, the influence of the Jewish matrix declined and a largely Law-free form of Christianity became dominant. It is unclear how long this process took, or how large the movement was at this stage. By the time of Nero, Christianity could be identified. It was large enough to come to the attention of the authorities who looked on the movement not as a Jewish phenomenon but as something distinct. 'Law-free' meant that the gentile Christians in Rome did not practise circumcision, and neither did they observe the dietary laws. The Roman view of the sabbath was that it was a sign of laziness that people did not work full-time.

A largely Law-free form of Christianity became dominant.

---

13. Suetonius: *Lives* – *Nero*, xvi.
14. Sulpicius Severus: *Chronicle*, ii.29.

Once the expulsion conducted by Claudius was relaxed – still in the time of Claudius – Christian Jews could return to Rome. This would have included the likes of Aquila and Priscilla. The returning Christian Jews expected to return to their former positions of prominence in the community, re-establishing the Jewish matrix and insisting upon circumcision, the dietary laws and Sabbath observance. But the newly prominent gentile Christians, having evolved their own law-free version of Christianity and who now perhaps filled the positions of authority, rejected their proposals. A conflict ensued, and this is the very conflict which the Letter to the Romans addresses.

After two thousand years of separation from Jewish identity markers, it is difficult for Christians today to have sympathy with the returnees. Each side had its position and its strength. A gentile could say to his or her fellow Christians, 'Our way is the more mature; we have discovered a freedom in Christ, according to which we are not obliged to keep the ritual Law. We are not going back to a position of inferiority.' Whereas a Jew could say to his or her fellow Christians, 'The Law was given directly by God to Moses, who wrote it down. It was never part of Christian identity that the Law could be suspended or abolished. On the contrary, the same God who gave us the Law also gave us the Messiah. In fact, Jesus the Messiah was one of us and came from our religion. We enjoy, therefore, a certain priority and primacy.' Naturally, such arguments did not remain at a level of intellectual exchange. The tendency on each side to look down on the other must have been very marked because Paul came back to it again and again. Some examples may illustrate this.

> Therefore you have no excuse, whoever you are, when you judge others; for in passing judgment on another you condemn yourself, because you, the judge, are doing the very same things. You say, "We know that God's judgment on those who do such things is in accordance with truth." Do you imagine, whoever you are, that when you judge those who do such things and yet do them yourself, you will escape the judgment of God? (Rom 2:1-4)

> What then? Are we any better off? No, not at all; for we have already charged that all, both Jews and Greeks, are under the power of sin, (Rom 3:9)

> Now I am speaking to you Gentiles. Inasmuch then as I am an apostle to the Gentiles, I glorify my ministry in order to make my own people jealous, and thus save some of them. For if their rejection is the reconciliation of the world, what will their acceptance be but life from the dead! If the part of the dough offered as first fruits is holy, then the whole batch is holy; and if the root is holy, then the branches also are holy. But if some of the branches were broken off, and you, a wild olive shoot, were grafted in their place to share the rich root of the olive tree, do not boast over the branches. If you do boast, remember that it is not you that support the root, but the root that supports you. You will say, 'Branches were broken off so that I might be grafted in.' That is true. They were broken off because of their unbelief, but you stand only through faith. So do not become proud, but stand in awe. For if God did not spare the natural branches, perhaps he will not spare you. (Rom 11:13-21)

> Welcome those who are weak in faith, but not for the purpose of quarrelling over opinions. Some believe in eating anything, while the weak eat only vegetables. Those who eat must not despise those who abstain, and those who abstain must not pass judgment on those who eat; for God has welcomed them. Who are you to pass judgment on servants of another? It is before their own lord that they stand or fall. And they will be upheld, for the Lord is able to make them stand. (Rom 14:1-4)

3.3   SUMMARY

a)   At the start, Christians were mostly Jews, with some gentiles.

b)   At a certain point, the Jewish Christians were expelled (not all Jews).

c)   The gentiles developed a law-free style of Christianity.

d)   On the return of the Jewish Christians, the community was in conflict.

e)   The conflict was fuelled by mutual disparagement.

EXERCISE 1:

a)   *How did the Roman people eventually distinguished Jews from Christians? Write 5 lines.*

b)   *What is the nature of the conflict between gentile and Jewish Christians at Rome? Write 5 lines.*

SECTION TWO:
THE PURPOSE AND STRUCTURE OF THE LETTER

I. PAUL'S AGENDA

I.I WHY IT MATTERED TO PAUL

The issues at Rome mattered greatly to Paul. His vision was that, in Christ, both Jews and gentiles were heirs to the promises to Abraham. Although he himself was the apostle to the gentiles, he was sharply aware that both parts of the Christian family belonged together. So much was this the case, that he organised the Jerusalem collection as a way to marking the mutual indebtedness of Jews and gentiles. Furthermore, as was seen in *Galatians*, for him both the inclusion of the gentiles and the dropping of all ethnic identity-markers stemmed directly from his understanding of the cross of Jesus, in the light of the resurrection. A great deal was at stake. Added to that, the fact that all this was happening in Rome, the capital of the empire, with lots of traffic to and fro, meant that the conflict was widely known and could have a wider effect. Paul was therefore keen that the community in the capital, with its history of Jews and gentiles, should resolve the conflict and thereby become an example of reconciliation and tolerance to the emerging Christian movement all over the empire.

I.2 A LETTER AND A SPEECH

It is relatively easy to identify the letter-form in *Romans*. It is more difficult to trace the rhetorical outlines. Careful delimitation is the key. This involves three initial steps:

a)   the typical vocabulary of a section;

b)   the frame, marking the beginning and the end; and

c)   the 'rivets', that is, the shared vocabulary facilitating the transition from the end of one unit to the beginning of another.

For each identifiable unit of argument there should be two sets of 'rivets', one at the start and one at the end. The results of such investigation can be presented schematically as follows (the details will be traced in each successive section of the comment).

Verses	Vocabulary	Frame	Rivets
1:16-4:25	Jew, Gentile, faith, ungodliness, unrighteousness.	1:16-17 faith, righteous, written	
		4:23-25 written, believe, justification	4:23-25 believe, our Lord Jesus Christ, justification
5-8	Sin, Christ, life, live, salvation	5:1 God, our Lord Jesus Christ	5:1-2 justified, faith, our Lord Jesus Christ
		8:39 God, Christ Jesus our Lord.	8:39 separate, Christ
9-11	Sarah, Jacob, Esau, Moses, Abraham, Hosea, Benjamin, Elijah, and Israelite	9:4-5 covenant, forever and ever. Amen.	9:1-2 Christ, anathema
		11:27,36 covenant, forever and ever. Amen.	11:25 not wiser, 11:30-31 mercy; 36 ages, God
12:1-15:6	self, one another, neighbour and brother and sister	12:1 I encourage you; God ('worship')	12:1 mercies, 2 this age, 3 not more highly, God
		15:5-6 God, encouragement ('worship')	15:5-6 Christ, one another, glorify, God
			15:7 Christ, one another, glory, God

Such a careful delimitation permits an initial identification of the progress of *Romans* as follows:

Verse	Moment	Topic
1:8-15	Introduction	Reasons for coming to Rome
1:16-17	Thesis	Faith, justification, salvation, Jews, gentiles
1:18-4:25	Proof 1	The need of Christ
5-8	Proof 2	The gift of life in Christ
9-11	Proof 3	God's election of Jews and gentiles
12:1-15:6	Proof 4	Living together in the community
15:7-33	Conclusion	Summary and travel plans

The development of the argument all springs from the thesis in 1:16-17.

Thesis: Rom 1:16-17	Language	Topic
Power of God for salvation	5-8: justification and salvation	Gift of justification to the Christian community
Everyone who has faith	1-4: justification, Jew, Gentile	Powerlessness of both Jew and Gentile, the coming of faith
To the Jew first and then the Greek	9-11: Israelites and Gentiles in God's plan for human history	Priority of Judaism and the new position of the Gentiles
The one who is righteous will live by faith	12-15: mutually, body, belonging together	Practical advice on how to live together with integrity and tolerance

Finally, it is possible to combine the schemas as follows:

Verse	Letter	Rhetoric	Topic
1:1-7	Superscript		Sender, addresses, greetings
1:8-15	Thanksgiving	Introduction	Reasons for coming to Rome
1:16-17	Body	Thesis	Faith, salvation, righteousness
1:18-4:25		Proof 1	Need before God
5-8		Proof 2	Salvation in Christ
9-11		Proof 3	Place of both Jew and gentile
12:1-15:6		Proof 4	Tolerance and integrity
15:7-33		Conclusion	Summary, reasons for coming to Rome
16	Postscript		Greetings to twenty-six people and a prayer

2. CONCLUSION

A number of conclusions, even at this early stage, seem important.

2.1 JEWISH RITUAL LAW

There was a major problem which divided the Roman Christian communities. It involved the observance of the Jewish Law, in particular the ritual law (circumcision, dietary laws and Sabbath observance). Christianity had slowly become identifiable as a separate movement from Judaism. Scholars propose a particular history to explain both the emergence of Christianity in Rome and the writing of the *Letter to the Romans*.

2.2 PAUL'S KNOWLEDGE

As the apostle to the gentiles, what was going on in Rome mattered greatly to Paul. He wrote his *Letter to the Romans* to a church he had not founded, to give them his theological reasoning and practical advice. Although he had never been there, it is clear that he had his finger on the pulse, because at the very end of the letter, he was able to name no fewer than twenty-six people who were present.

The *Letter to the Romans* can be analysed as a letter and as a speech (rhetoric). It would have been possible for Paul to have written a much shorter letter, perhaps just the thanksgiving, together with most of chapters 12 to 15, and then added the greetings at the end. However, Paul honoured the Romans by giving them an extensive and deep treatment of the issues. In the first three proofs, the grounds are given for the practical advice provided in the fourth proof. The order of the persuasion is itself instructive. He begins by demolishing the

Paul honoured the Romans by giving them an extensive and deep treatment of the issues.

UNIT SEVEN
SECTION TWO

superiority of each side (Proof 1): there is 'no distinction'. He continues by showing just how much each side shares with the other (Proof 2): there is to be a large family. Naturally, the question of Jewish identity in history and the substantial Jewish rejection of Jesus gave rise to difficult questions which Paul dealt with in chapters 9 to 11 (Proof 3). Finally, the advice is given (Proof 4).

Once the order is appreciated, it is clear that no other way of proceeding would have been as powerful. The advice must wait until the end. The relationship of Jew and gentile, already an issue in *Romans* 3, can be examined only in the light of Christ. Finally, while Paul could have started with Christ (Proof 2), that would have meant moving on to moral failure (Proof 1), from which it might have been difficult to move forward. So, complex though *Romans* undoubtedly is, the overall sequence seems logical enough.

For pedagogical reasons, the examination of *Romans* 1:1-15,16-17 is postponed until the overall letter has been fully looked at.

EXERCISE 2:

a) *Describe the rhetorical lay-out of the* Letter to the Romans *as a whole. Write 5 lines.*

b) *Explain why, in the* Letter to the Romans, *the practical advice comes last. Write 5 lines.*

SECTION THREE:
ROMANS 1-4

Fig. 25: *Remains of the Roman forum, with the Colosseum in background*

1. INTRODUCTION

Romans 1-4 explores the human hunger for help and direction in life. Nowadays believers are under considerable pressure from books, media and public figures to let go of their out-dated convictions. One of the tasks facing Christians today is to explore – at a personal and community level – these dimensions of faith:

*   Why do I / we believe at all?

*   What difference does believing make to me / us?

*   How does faith spring from one's experience of life?

Some aspects of this modern quest are opened up in *Romans* 1-4. Paul talks about how the Creator can be known from the creation. Again, in a long reflection on moral achievement, or rather its opposite, he teaches that the need for something more in our lives is palpable. All of this can be of help to us today.

2. ROMANS 1:16-4:25

2.1 DELIMITATION

The delimitation of the section can help greatly in discovering the issues and topics encountered in these chapters.

a)   *Vocabulary*

A striking feature of the *Letter to the Romans* is the spread of vocabulary to do with Jews and gentiles.

1-4	5-8	9-11	12-16
20	0	10	10

From this it can be learned that in 1-4 Paul talks especially about Jews and gentiles. Furthermore, while the vocabulary of justification / to justify does not set 1-4 apart from 5-8, nevertheless, 1-4 is marked by the language of unrighteousness / faith / unfaith / believe / godliness.

b)   Frames

At the beginning and end of the section there is a notable frame, or inclusion.

1:16 For I am not ashamed of the gospel; it is the power of God for salvation to everyone who has **faith**, to the Jew first and also to the Greek. ¹⁷For in it the **righteousness** of God is revealed through **faith** for **faith**; as it is **written**, 'The one who is **righteous** will live by **faith**'.	4:23 Now the words, 'it was reckoned to him', were **written** not for his sake alone, ²⁴but for ours also. It will be reckoned to us who **believe** in him who raised Jesus our Lord from the dead, ²⁵who was handed over to death for our trespasses and was raised for our **justification**.

c)   Rivets

Finally, there is a bridge at the end of chapter 4 anticipating the vocabulary of chapter 5.

4:23 Now the words, 'it was reckoned to him,' were written not for his sake alone, ²⁴but for ours also. It will be reckoned to us who **believe** in him who raised **Jesus our Lord** from the dead, ²⁵who was handed over to death for our trespasses and was raised for our **justification**.	5:1 Therefore, since we are **justified** by **faith**, we have peace with God through **our Lord Jesus Christ**, ²through whom we have obtained access to this grace in which we stand; and we boast in our hope of sharing the glory of God.

2.2   STRUCTURE

Within the overall persuasion of *Romans*, this passage relates to the other units as follows:

Rom 1-4	Rom 5-8	Rom 9-11	Rom 12:1-15:6
No distinction	A large family	No Distinction	Welcome others
Gentile and Jew in need before God	All believers receive abundantly	Inclusion of Israel	Live inclusively!

The layout of 1:16-4:25 seems clear enough.

i.   Idolatry and immorality (1:18-32)

ii   Judging others / God shows no partiality (2:1-29)

iii   Is there an advantage in being a Jew? (3:1-20)

iv   The faith of Abraham and our justification (3:21-4:25)

The thesis in 1:16-17 governs all the persuasion in *Romans* and in particular this persuasion here.

Thesis	1:16-17	Justification by faith.
Proof 1	Subthesis 1:18	Idolatry and immorality *gentiles are held responsible*
Proof 2	Subthesis 2:1	Judging others: God shows no partiality *Jews are held responsible*
Proof 3	Subthesis 3:1	Is there any advantage in being a Jew? *Yes and No! Not really.*
Proof 4	Subthesis 3:21-22	Faith *Jews and gentiles (in that order!) have* *access to justification by faith.* *Argument from Abraham.*

Given that one cannot treat all of 1-4 in detail, the comments below on selected verses will illustrate the development of the argument.

3. KEY MOMENTS IN ROMANS

3.1 IDOLATRY AND IMMORALITY

Romans 1:18-32

As Paul faced a divided community, his first challenge was to demolish any sense of moral superiority on either side. He does this first of all by reminding the gentiles of their background in idolatry and immorality. It may seem unkind of Paul to begin with the guests, but there was a double advantage in this:

• the Christian gentiles, broadly, were the 'strong', and would be able to sustain the abuse; and

• the Christian Jews were being involuntarily led to judge the gentiles, and were then condemned for judging. Thus, Paul reminds one group of its weakness and, in a way, tricks the other group into exposing its weakness.

Paul's argument begins with the failure of the gentiles, while still outside the faith, to come to an adequate knowledge of God. Following teachings found also in the *Wisdom of Solomon*, Paul teaches that the Creator may be known from the created but that, instead, people made up the silliest of idols and treated them as gods (a mortal human being or birds or four-footed animals or reptiles). This was standard Jewish invective against pagan idolatry. Even at this point, the Jews in the Roman communities must have been feeling that Paul was on their side, really. The apostle then goes on to make a connection between idolatry and immorality. Without an adequate theology, the morality of the pagans went completely awry. A very graphic account of the consequences may be found towards the end of the section.

Without an adequate theology, the morality of the pagans went completely awry.

> [28]And since they did not see fit to acknowledge God, God gave them up to a debased mind and to things that should not be done. [29]They were filled with every kind of wickedness, evil, covetousness, malice. Full of envy, murder, strife, deceit, craftiness, they are gossips, [30]slanderers, God-haters, insolent, haughty, boastful, inventors of evil, rebellious toward parents, [31]foolish, faithless, heartless, ruthless. [32]They know God's decree, that those who practice such things deserve to die – yet they not only do them but even applaud others who practice them. (Rom 1:28-32)

In an emotional piling up of juicy accusations, the apostle warms to his theme. How would the gentiles have been feeling at this point? How would the Jews have been feeling? The gentiles would have experienced a tension between guilt and relief. Guilt because their past was fearlessly exposed; relief because it was their past. As converts, they would have made a journey away from that idolatry and immorality. At this point, the Jews may well have been feeling that at last an influential apostle, one of their own, had put the gentiles in their place. It is true, of course, that Jews could not be accused of crass idolatry. However, when it comes to morality, it is another question altogether, to which Paul then turned.

3.2   JUDGING OTHERS
Romans 2:1-29

Without further ado, Paul, having inveigled the Jewish Christians into judgement and self-satisfaction, attacks anyone who judges another: 'Do you imagine, whoever you are, that when you judge those who do such things and yet do them yourself, you will escape the judgment of God?' (Rom 2:3-4). In reality, all have sinned, both those who have the written Law of Moses and those who have the Law written on their hearts. Then follows an electrifying passage designed to cause maximum discomfort:

> [17]But if you call yourself a Jew and rely on the law and boast of your relation to God [18]and know his will and determine what is best because you are instructed in the law, [19]and if you are sure that you are a guide to the blind, a light to those who are in darkness, [20]a corrector of the foolish, a teacher of children, having in the law the embodiment of knowledge and truth, [21]you, then, that teach others, will you not teach yourself? While you preach against stealing, do you steal? [22]You that forbid adultery, do you commit adultery? You that abhor idols, do you rob temples? [23]You that boast in the law, do you dishonour God by breaking the law? [24]For, as it is written, 'The name of God is blasphemed among the Gentiles because of you.' (Rom 2:17-24)

Just as Paul had earlier detailed the moral failings of the gentiles, so here Paul lists the self congratulation of the Jews before detailing in turn their moral failings. Naturally, no one in the congregation could deny that he or she breaks the Law (theft, adultery, robbing temples and the like). The contrast between the high moral ground (always a place of dangerous exposure) and the low moral reality is meant to be penetrating and painful.

The apostle then draws out a principle which would be even more upsetting:

> [25]Circumcision indeed is of value if you obey the law; but if you break the law, your circumcision has become uncircumcision. [26]So, if those who are uncircumcised keep the requirements of the law, will not their uncircumcision be regarded as circumcision? [27]Then those who are physically uncircumcised but keep the law will condemn you that have the written code and circumcision but break the law. [28]For a person is not a Jew who is one outwardly, nor is true circumcision something external and physical. [29]Rather, a person is a Jew who is one inwardly, and real circumcision is a matter of the heart – it is spiritual and not literal. Such a person receives praise not from others but from God. (Rom 2:25-29)

It is in verses 28-29 that the heart of what Paul is trying to say is found. Everyone really knows the moral law – Jews from the Law, gentiles from conscience. Everyone really sins and will face judgement. A Jew who keeps the Law and the gentile who follows conscience are equally in good standing before God and will receive praise, not from humans, but from God, the only judge.

Naturally, such an argument gives rise to another question: If that is the case, what is the point of being Jewish at all? Paul, fearless logician that he is, turns to this question next.

3.3   AN ADVANTAGE IN BEING JEWISH?

Romans 3:1-20

Fig. 26: *Arch of Titus – relief depicting the triumph of Titus in Rome*

In this passage there are two answers given to the same question, and they seem to contradict one another.

> Then what advantage has the Jew? Or what is the value of circumcision? Much, in every way. For in the first place the Jews were entrusted with the oracles of God. (Rom 3:1-2)

> What then? Are we any better off? No, not at all; for we have already charged that all, both Jews and Greeks, are under the power of sin. (Rom 3:9)

The ambiguity is part of Paul's case. Naturally, he wanted to affirm that God's choice of the Jewish people was historical, and still stands. He would come back to that again in a very pained passage in *Romans 9*:

> They were Israelites, and to them belong the adoption, the glory, the covenants, the giving of the law, the worship, and the promises; to them belong the patriarchs, and from them, according to the flesh, comes the Messiah, who is over all, God blessed forever. Amen. (Rom 9:4-5)

At the same time, Paul needed to show that both Jew and gentile stand in need of what was achieved for us in Christ. The chief evidence for that is their moral failure, in which there is also 'no distinction'! He wanted to say that at one level Jews were special, and at another level, they are the same as everyone else. As in the case against the gentiles, he warms to his theme and appends a devastating series of quotations from scripture, that is, from the Word of God, to show that not only have Jews failed but also that their failure has led gentiles away from God. It is very harsh. How would Christian Jews feel at this point? Like the gentiles earlier, they may have felt both guilt and relief. Guilt, because this was being said of God's chosen people; relief, because they have realised that something new has happened in Christ. It may be that this persuasion triggered a sense of detachment from the Jews, and therefore from the ritual Law, which marks out Judaism. That sense of having moved on may contribute to Paul's larger case in *Romans*. He summarises thus:

Paul needed to show that both Jew and gentile stand in need of what was achieved for us in Christ.

> Now we know that whatever the law says, it speaks to those who are under the law, so that every mouth may be silenced, and the whole world may be held accountable to God. For 'no human being will be justified in his sight' by deeds prescribed by the law, for through the law comes the knowledge of sin. (Rom 3:19-20)

Thus Paul lays out the universal need of Christ.

3.4   ABRAHAM AND OUR JUSTIFICATION

Romans 3:21-4:25

Before this long passage can be appreciated, a translation issue must be faced. In the NRSV, one reads:

> But now, apart from law, the righteousness of God has been disclosed, and is attested by the law and the prophets, the righteousness of God through faith in Jesus Christ for all who believe. For there is no distinction, since all have sinned and fall short of the glory of God; they are now justified by his grace as a gift, through the redemption that is in Christ Jesus, whom God put forward as a sacrifice of atonement by his blood, effective through faith. He did this to show his righteousness, because in his divine forbearance he had passed over the sins previously committed; it was to prove at the present time that he himself is righteous and that he justifies the one who has faith in Jesus. (Rom 3:21-26)

Notice the expression 'faith in Jesus'. There is a large scholarly discussion about this expression because the word for faith in Greek can have two meanings: faith and faithfulness / fidelity. The translation printed above does not quite make sense as it stands, and some corrective adjustments are necessary. The genitive cases in Greek permit two readings,

- the faith we have in Jesus; or

- the faith Jesus himself had.

For reasons already explored in *Galatians*, the reading here will follow the second option, that is, the faith Jesus himself had. Adjusted, the text reads as follows:

> But now, apart from law, the righteousness of God has been disclosed, and is attested by the law and the prophets, the righteousness of God through the *faith/fidelity of Jesus Christ* for all who believe. For there is no distinction, since all have sinned and fall short of the glory of God; they are now justified by his grace as a gift, through the redemption that is in Christ Jesus, whom God put forward as a sacrifice of atonement by his blood, effective *through his faith/fidelity*. He did this to show his righteousness, because in his divine forbearance he had passed over the sins previously committed; it was to prove at the present time that he himself is righteous and that he justifies the one *who lives from the faith/fidelity of Jesus*. (Rom 3:21-26)

The gentiles knew by the law of conscience what was wrong.

The Jews knew by the Law of Moses what was wrong.

This is a very important moment in *Romans*. Until Christ came along, humans were effectively alone in the moral world. The gentiles knew by the law of conscience what was wrong, but sinned nevertheless. The Jews knew by the Law of Moses what was wrong, but transgressed nevertheless. Now God has put in place, not regulations, but a relationship which enables humans to stand before God as God wants them to be. The faith / fidelity of Jesus is offered as *our relationship to the Father*, and, thus empowered, both Jews and gentiles find themselves enabled to live the moral law.

As he had done before in *Galatians*, Paul then calls up the example of Abraham who was justified because he had faith. As in the case of Abraham, the key words are faith, gift and promise. For Jewish Christians, who have made the journey to faith in Christ, there can be no grounds whatever for boasting. They may indeed be direct descendants of Abraham according to the flesh, but the gentiles are also his descendants according to the promise. Any sense of superiority, either from Jew or gentile, is thereby excluded.

⁹Is this blessedness, then, pronounced only on the circumcised, or also on the uncircumcised? We say, 'Faith was reckoned to Abraham as righteousness.' ¹⁰How then was it reckoned to him? Was it before or after he had been circumcised? It was not after, but before he was circumcised. ¹¹He received the sign of circumcision as a seal of the righteousness that he had by faith while he was still uncircumcised. The purpose was to make him the ancestor of all who believe without being circumcised and who thus have righteousness reckoned to them, ¹²and likewise the ancestor of the circumcised who are not only circumcised but who also follow the example of the faith that our ancestor Abraham had before he was circumcised. (Rom 4:9-12)

4. CONCLUSIONS

These chapters have had a tremendous influence on later generations of Christians. Naturally, the argument style, especially in chapter 4, is very Jewish and somewhat foreign to us. But to persuade the Christian Jews in Rome, Paul has to speak their language. His hope was that he had said enough to expose a common need of God in Christ and to show that both Jews and gentiles belong *without distinction*, precisely because *God shows no partiality*. To summarise the argument thus far:

God shows no partiality.

- the need for God is experienced by both gentiles and Jews;

- 'there is no distinction', certainly in moral achievement;

- the real circumcision is the moral life, written on the human heart;

- God offers salvation through the faith of Jesus; and

- we all access it through the faith we have in Jesus.

The next step will be a more positive one: What are the gifts we have all received without distinction, in the light of which Jews and gentiles should be able to live together?

EXERCISE 3:

a) *Describe Paul's approach to both gentiles and Jews in* Romans 1-4. *Write 5 lines.*

b) *Describe the argument from Abraham as used in* Romans 3-4. *Write 5 lines.*

SECTION FOUR:
ROMANS 5-8

Fig. 27: *Fresco of Adam and Eve found in the Roman catacombs*

1.   INTRODUCTION

Chapters 5-8 of *Romans* are brimful of ideas, and it can be difficult to make one's way around the text. These challenges are literary and theological. In this unit, *Romans* 5-8 will be looked at first as a whole, and then one particular passage of special significance will be examined in detail. Why *Romans* 5:1-21? This particular passage has had a tremendous – some would say disproportionate – influence on church teaching, especially since the time of Augustine.

In these chapters, Paul continues the reflection achieved in *Romans* 1-4, but goes on from there to speak of the universal need of salvation, of Christ. It is not so much a change of topic as an initial deepening. The beginning of *Romans* 5-8 takes Paul to a reflection on Adam and Original Sin. Putting it very succinctly, the topic is two-fold:

a)   our need of God as revealed in Christ; and

b)   God's love revealed in Christ.

Paul's insight is that the extent of human need before God was not so clear until Christ came.

God's love is revealed in Christ. But part of Paul's insight is that the extent of human need before God was not so clear until Christ came. Paul, in a way, works backwards from the cure to the disease. In the light of Christ, he is able to use the Adam story to explore the human condition. Big issues are at stake here:

*   the human condition;

*   redemption in Christ; and

*   the love of God.

2.   THE DELIMITATION OF CHAPTERS 5-8

It is always helpful to say why any particular part of a text may be treated as a unit. The benefit ought to be a greater awareness of the nature of the text and better understanding of how this passage fits into the persuasion as a whole.

2.1   VOCABULARY

The vocabulary of these chapters changes the following:

Sin, transgression, Adam

1-4	5-8	9-11	12-16
14	58	1	6

Life, to live

1-4	5-8	9-11	12-16
2	24	0	11

Jesus Christ

1-4	5-8	9-11	12-16
18	38	9	37 (of which 13 in ch 16)

Our Lord Jesus Christ

1-4	5-8	9-11	12-16
8	25	0	9

There is also a marked increase in verbs in the first person plural. Even at a first glance, this tells us that Paul will be dealing with what affects all of us (the first person plural), that is sin, in the light of Christ through whom we have life.

2.2   FRAMES

Paul frames his discourse with an echo of the beginning of chapter 5 at the end of chapter 8.

Therefore, since we are justified by *faith*, we have peace with **God** through **our Lord Jesus Christ**, through whom we have obtained access to this grace in which we stand; and we boast in our *hope* of sharing the glory of God. (Rom 5:1-2)	For I am convinced that neither death, nor life, nor angels, nor rulers, nor things present, nor things to come, nor powers, nor height, nor depth, nor anything else in all creation, will be able to separate us from the *love* of **God** in **Christ Jesus our Lord**. (Rom 8:38-39)

The word 'God' is everywhere in *Romans* and hardly sets the section apart. However, combined with the full expression 'Our Lord Jesus Christ', which really does set all of chapters 5-8 apart, one has a frame. Finally, that Pauline triad – faith, hope and love – is partially present at the beginning and end of *Romans* 5-9, mapping something of the journey of the passage.

2.3   RIVETS

For **I am convinced** that neither death, nor life, nor angels, nor rulers, nor things present, nor things to come, nor powers, nor height, nor depth, nor anything else in all creation, will be able to *separate* us from the love of God in **Christ** Jesus our Lord. (Rom 8:38-39)	**I am speaking the truth** in **Christ** – I am not lying; my conscience confirms it by the Holy Spirit – I have great sorrow and unceasing anguish in my heart. For I could wish that I myself were accursed and *cut off* from **Christ** for the sake of my own people, my kindred according to the flesh. (Rom 9:1-3)

Thus, at the end of chapter 8, Paul prepares the reader / hearer for the shock of 9:1-3. He changes from the more usual first person plural to the first person singular. 'I am convinced' is echoed in 'I am speaking the truth'. Finally, 'separate' is matched by '[cut] off from'.

EXERCISE 4:

a) *Describe the main topics of* Romans *5-8. Write 5 lines.*

b) *Describe the delimitation of* Romans *5-8. Write 5 lines.*

2.4 STRUCTURE

In terms of the overall structure, this is the Second Proof, subject as always to the thesis of 1:16-17

> For I am not ashamed of the gospel; it is the power of God for salvation to everyone who has faith, to the Jew first and also to the Greek. For in it the righteousness of God is revealed through faith for faith; as it is written, 'The one who is righteous will live by faith.' (Rom 1:16-17)

The particular dimension explored in *Romans* 5-8 is 'the power of God for salvation'. The noun 'salvation' and the verb 'to save' are not found that frequently in *Romans* (only thirteen times in all). However, the only occurrences in chapters 5-8 (in the passive first person plural) do have a kind of thematic function.

> Much more surely then, now that we have been justified by his blood, will we be saved through him from the wrath of God. For if while we were enemies, we were reconciled to God through the death of his Son, much more surely, having been reconciled, will we be saved by his life. (Rom 5:9-10)

> For in hope we were saved. Now hope that is seen is not hope. For who hopes for what is seen? (Rom 8:24)

Within these chapters, there is what seems to be a clear chronological pattern in the issues treated:

Rom 5.	Salvation / justification in Christ	
	Faith	
Rom 6.	Baptism	Sanctification
Rom 7.	The law of God and the law of sin	
Rom 8.	Prayer	Father – Abba
		The Spirit – intercession
		Christ – unshakeable hope

Paul seems to move in these chapters from the human condition, expressed in Adam, through the gift of salvation in Christ, towards the hope of final redemption. In between, he names the journey: faith leading to baptism, sanctification and the inner struggle, prayer to Abba, in the Spirit, through Christ.

Paul named the journey: faith leading to baptism, sanctification and the inner struggle, prayer to Abba, in the Spirit, through Christ.

One of the great themes of *Romans* is that there is 'no distinction' between Jew and Greek. The overall task of *Romans* 1-4 is to show that, in spite of everything, all equally sin. The overall task of *Romans* 5-8 is to show just how much all have received in Christ. The universal need of salvation is summed up in the Adam story; then Paul follows up with a chronologically arranged account of all we have received in Christ, both in the past, in the present and in the future. If on the basis of one's need, one can say 'there is no distinction', all the more so, on the basis of gift, can one say, 'there is no distinction' at all:

> For those whom he foreknew he also predestined to be conformed to the image of his Son, in order that he might be the firstborn among many brothers. (Rom 8:29; ESV; 'Among many brothers' is rendered inclusively in the NRSV as 'within a large family').

As it is not feasible to examine every moment in the text, the commentary below will be limited to *Romans* 5:1-21.

3.   COMMENTARY ON ROMANS 5:1-21

At this stage, students are invited to read this passage and formulate questions for later reflection.

> ¹Therefore, since we are justified by faith, we have peace with God through our Lord Jesus Christ, ²through whom we have obtained access to this grace in which we stand; and we boast in our hope of sharing the glory of God. ³And not only that, but we also boast in our sufferings, knowing that suffering produces endurance, ⁴and endurance produces character, and character produces hope, ⁵and hope does not disappoint us, because God's love has been poured into our hearts through the Holy Spirit that has been given to us. (Rom 5:1-5)

> ⁶For while we were still weak, at the right time Christ died for the ungodly. ⁷Indeed, rarely will anyone die for a righteous person – though perhaps for a good person someone might actually dare to die. ⁸But God proves his love for us in that while we still were sinners Christ died for us. ⁹Much more surely then, now that we have been justified by his blood, will we be saved through him from the wrath of God. ¹⁰For if while we were enemies, we were reconciled to God through the death of his Son, much more surely, having been reconciled, will we be saved by his life. ¹¹But more than that, we even boast in God through our Lord Jesus Christ, through whom we have now received reconciliation. (Rom 5:6-11)

> ¹²Therefore, just as sin came into the world through one man, and death came through sin, and so death spread to all because all have sinned – ¹³sin was indeed in the world before the law, but sin is not reckoned when there is no law. ¹⁴Yet death exercised dominion from Adam to Moses, even over those whose sins were not like the transgression of Adam, who is a type of the one who was to come. (Rom 5:12-14)

[15]But the free gift is not like the trespass. For if the many died through the one man's trespass, much more surely have the grace of God and the free gift in the grace of the one man, Jesus Christ, abounded for the many. [16]And the free gift is not like the effect of the one man's sin. For the judgment following one trespass brought condemnation, but the free gift following many trespasses brings justification. [17]If, because of the one man's trespass, death exercised dominion through that one, much more surely will those who receive the abundance of grace and the free gift of righteousness exercise dominion in life through the one man, Jesus Christ. (Rom 5:15-17)

[18]Therefore just as one man's trespass led to condemnation for all, so one man's act of righteousness leads to justification and life for all. [19]For just as by the one man's disobedience the many were made sinners, so by the one man's obedience the many will be made righteous. [20]But law came in, with the result that the trespass multiplied; but where sin increased, grace abounded all the more, [21]so that, just as sin exercised dominion in death, so grace might also exercise dominion through justification leading to eternal life through Jesus Christ our Lord. (Rom 5:18-21)

Students may find it helpful to think of the following, in advance:

a)   Paul assumes the historicity of Adam.

b)   The worldview is apocalyptic, one dimension of which is the conviction that the beginning (creation) and the end (*eschaton*) would resemble each other.

c)   Once again, justification means, in brief, 'right relationship'.

d)   Sin is regarded as a force in the world.

e)   Many terms are used to explore the meaning of Jesus' death.

f)   On a literary level, at verse 12, Paul interrupts himself and inserts a long and highly significant reflection (verses 13-17), before continuing the original line of thought from verse 12 to verse 18. This does make the text difficult to read.

3.1   ROMANS 5:1-5

[1]Therefore, since we are justified by faith, we have peace with God through our Lord Jesus Christ, [2]through whom we have obtained access to this grace in which we stand; and we boast in our hope of sharing the glory of God. [3]And not only that, but we also boast in our sufferings, knowing that suffering produces endurance, [4]and endurance produces character, and character produces hope, [5]and hope does not disappoint us, because God's love has been poured into our hearts through the Holy Spirit that has been given to us. (Rom 5:1-5)

In verse 1a, by mentioning justification, Paul makes a deft link with the previous four chapters. He then introduces, still in a general way, the gifts of grace, expressed as faith, hope and love – that great Pauline triad. Finally, the reader will not fail to notice the incipiently Trinitarian background in the passage: God, our Lord Jesus Christ and the Holy Spirit. The word 'peace' mentioned at the start means peace with God in the apocalyptic context of 'wrath', but also peace with each other in the reception of the gifts of salvation. On a more literary, rhetorical note, verses 3-5a are in the rhetorical form of 'climax', with one element leading to another. Perhaps one can see here the whole chronological sequence of *Romans 5-8* anticipated *in nuce*.

3.2   ROMANS 5:6-11

⁶For while we were still weak, at the right time Christ died for the ungodly. ⁷Indeed, rarely will anyone die for a righteous person – though perhaps for a good person someone might actually dare to die. ⁸But God proves his love for us in that while we still were sinners Christ died for us. ⁹Much more surely then, now that we have been justified by his blood, will we be saved through him from the wrath of God. ¹⁰For if while we were enemies, we were reconciled to God through the death of his Son, much more surely, having been reconciled, will we be saved by his life. ¹¹But more than that, we even boast in God through our Lord Jesus Christ, through whom we have now received reconciliation. (Rom 5:6-11)

ungodly
sinners
enemies

This remarkable passage describes the human condition and the gift of redemption in a complex variety of metaphors. The condition before salvation is described as: ungodly, sinners, enemies. The gift in Christ is described as: 'for us', justified by his blood, saved (twice), reconciled and reconciliation. The words 'death' and 'life' are also used. The words 'love' and 'wrath' are associated with God, words which seem contradictory today but which, in the apocalyptic worldview, were not so distant from each other.

Paul has before his eyes both the cross and the resurrection. 'For us' and 'blood' suggest to us the language of sacrifice, and they express the cost and the benefit of salvation. However, in the light of Paul's earlier teaching in *Galatians*, the background here is not one of sacrifice or propitiation to offset God's anger, but rather a communion sacrifice, by means of which people – specifically Jews and gentiles – are brought together in the peace of Christ. There was indeed a death, a death of compassionate solidarity with the human condition as an expression of God's unbounded, surprising love.

Paul remains, of course, an apocalyptic Jew who sees the world as coming to an end. At the very end, God's energy for justice – God's wrath – will be apparent, and believers are strengthened for that day by Jesus' death and resurrection. Verse 10 is significant. In the Pauline view, working back from the resurrection, believers are saved by the (risen) life of Jesus. In the light of the resurrection, Paul himself saw that the cross was really reconciliation, that is, reconciliation with God – through God's love – and reconciliation with each other – through Jesus' solidarity. The reconciliation of the cross was appreciated by Paul himself only in the light of his own encounter with the risen Jesus. The careful formulation in verse 10 mirrors his own journey of faith.

The reconciliation of the cross was appreciated by Paul himself only in the light of his own encounter with the risen Jesus.

3.3 ROMANS 5:12

> [12]Therefore, just as sin came into the world through one man, and death came through sin, and so death spread to all because all have sinned. (Rom 5:12)

As noted above, the continuation of these ideas is to be found in verse 18:

> Therefore just as one man's trespass led to condemnation for all, so one man's act of righteousness leads to justification and life for all. For just as by the one man's disobedience the many were made sinners, so by the one man's obedience the many will be made righteous. (Rom 5:18-19)

The translation of the last four words – 'because all have sinned' – is accurate, but historically there was an important problem with that text. The Greek version of the passage means, 'in as much as, all sinned'. However, the very influential Vulgate translated the passage as *in quo omnes peccaverunt*, which means, 'in whom all sinned'. According to the Greek, the cause of the spread of what was later called Original Sin was the further sinning of all humans. However, according to the Latin, the cause was the head of the human race who, in his role as the first human being, sinned. In an attempt to reconstruct the thought of Paul, the modern reader must follow the Greek, *pace* the western theological tradition.

In this whole passage, Paul presupposes a tradition that sees Adam's sin as the cause of death in the human race (Gen 3:19; 2 Esdr 3:7; 2 Apoc; Bar 17:2-3;23:4;48:42-43; Bib. Ant. 13:8; see 2 Enoch 30:16). Some forms of the tradition blame Eve (Sir 25:24; Apoc Mos 14) or the devil (Wis 2:23-24).

 Original Sin

There is far less evidence in Romans for the idea of Original Sin, though there is something like it in 4 Ezra (= 2 Esdras), which reads:

> *For a grain of evil seed was sown in Adam's heart from the beginning, and how much ungodliness it has produced until now – and will produce until the time of threshing comes! Consider now for yourself how much fruit of ungodliness a grain of evil seed has produced. When heads of grain without number are sown, how great a threshing floor they will fill! (2 Esd 4:30-32)*

The reader will notice that Paul has moved from Abraham back to Adam, and one can only ask: Why? There was a risk that his readers and hearers might think that the need for salvation was not universal and that in the period before the Law was given (which made transgression possible), people could not be held responsible. Paul replies by going back to the Adam story, which unleashed the power of sin in the world, causing death. This means that although they did not have the Law in the period between Adam and Moses, people still sinned, even though that sin was not exactly a transgression. So, sin and death are indeed universal, and so is the need for salvation. In the text of *Romans* 5, the thought begun in verse 12 continued in verse 18, as shall be seen:

Sin and death are indeed universal, and so is the need for salvation.

> [12]Therefore, just as sin came into the world through one man, and death came through sin, and so death spread to all because all have sinned. (Rom 5:12)

> [18]Therefore just as one man's trespass led to condemnation for all, so one man's act of righteousness leads to justification and life for all. (Rom 5:18)

At this point, Paul interrupts himself in an extended reflection, which will now be dealt with.

3.4 ROMANS 5:13-17

Clarification 1: Why do people still die?

> [13]Sin was indeed in the world before the law, but sin is not reckoned when there is no law. [14]Yet death exercised dominion from Adam to Moses, even over those whose sins were not like the transgression of Adam, who is a type of the one who was to come. (Rom 5:13-14)

Clarification 2: What was different about the one who was to come?

> [15]But the free gift is not like the trespass. For if the many died through the one man's trespass, much more surely have the grace of God and the free gift in the grace of the one man, Jesus Christ, abounded for the many. [16]And the free gift is not like the effect of the one man's sin. For the judgment following one trespass brought condemnation, but the free gift following many trespasses brings justification. (Rom 5:15-16)

Clarification 3: What was the different effect in Christ?

> [17]If, because of the one man's trespass, death exercised dominion through that one, much more surely will those who receive the abundance of grace and the free gift of righteousness exercise dominion in life through the one man, Jesus Christ. (Rom 5:17)

Paul offers a digression to explain the presence of sin and death, even in the in-between period. Sin was indeed present, although not reckoned because there was no explicit Law. Nevertheless, death, seen as a punishment for Adam's sin in *Genesis* 2-3, came to all. Thus all were indeed under the power of sin and death and so all needed salvation.

Romans 5:15-17 is a series of contrasts which depend on the apocalyptic conviction that the beginning and the end should resemble each other. Thus the congruence and incongruence of what happened in Adam and in Christ is presented in the literary form of an *a fortiori* (all the more so) argument. The contrasts can then be extracted:

Adam	Christ
One man	One man
Trespass	Free gift
Many died	Grace abounded for the many
Condemnation	Justification
Death	Life

Fig. 28: *Adam and Christ*

The frequent use of the word 'grace' is very noticeable here.

> [15]But the free gift is not like the trespass. For if the many died through the one man's trespass, much more surely have the grace of God and the free gift in the grace of the one man, Jesus Christ, abounded for the many. [16]And the free gift is not like the effect of the one man's sin. For the judgment following one trespass brought condemnation, but the free gift following many trespasses brings justification. [17]If, because of the one man's trespass, death exercised dominion through that one, much more surely will those who receive the abundance of grace and the free gift of righteousness exercise dominion in life through the one man, Jesus Christ. (Rom 5:15-17)

Note on the words used

Paul uses three words which are very close in meaning:

- 'Charis' (v.15 twice, v.17) means favour, good will, gift;

- 'Dorēma' and 'Dorea' mean gift or present. The NRSV has consistently added the word 'free' to make the meaning clear, perhaps following a hint in the King James Version.

Christ has made up for, and more than made up for, Adam's sin. The modern reader will wonder about the validity of the argument from Adam in the light of evolution and what we know scientifically about the origins of the human race. It should be said that Paul himself remained convinced, of course, of the historicity of the Adam story. But bear in mind that his purpose was to underline the universal power of sin and death, and the universal need for grace. It would be sufficient today to read the Adam story as a description of the human condition rather than an explanation of its cause. In this way, one can remain faithful to Paul's main object – which is to proclaim what happened in Christ. In fact, it may be added that Paul realised the need/flaw in humanity only in the light of what happened in Christ. Without being too naïve, one may say that he works back from the cure (the cross and resurrection of Jesus) to the condition (the universal power of sin and death). This may account for the absence of a doctrine of Original Sin in Judaism, although Jews also read *Genesis* 2-3.

It would be sufficient today to read the Adam's story as a description of the human condition rather than an explanation of its cause.

3.5   ROMANS 5:18-21

[12]Therefore, just as sin came into the world through one man, and death came through sin, and so death spread to all because all have sinned. (Rom 5:12)

[18]Therefore just as one man's trespass led to condemnation for all, so one man's act of righteousness leads to justification and life for all. [19]For just as by the one man's disobedience the many were made sinners, so by the one man's obedience the many will be made righteous. [20]But law came in, with the result that the trespass multiplied; but where sin increased, grace abounded all the more, [21]so that, just as sin exercised dominion in death, so grace might also exercise dominion through justification leading to eternal life through Jesus Christ our Lord. (Rom 5:18-21)

It is helpful to read verse 12 here to get the sense of continuity after the digression. The comparisons continue in verses 18-19. In verse 20, Paul comes back to his worry about the Law. People did indeed sin before the Law came, that is, they did what was wrong. But it could not be said that they transgressed, because what was wrong was not forbidden by commandment. When the Law did come, sin became transgression. The advantage of the Law was that it identified what was wrong. The disadvantage of the Law was that it could not help people keep it and, from a certain point of view, made them more responsible: so it may be said that 'transgression multiplied'. Paul elsewhere reflected on sin as a kind of spiritual force which took advantage of this weakness inherent in the Law, making the human condition even worse.

When the Law did come, sin became transgression.

The advantage of the Law was that it identified what was wrong. The disadvantage of the Law was that it could not help people keep it, and from a certain point of view made them more responsible.

> What then should we say? That the law is sin? By no means! Yet, if it had not been for the law, I would not have known sin. I would not have known what it is to covet if the law had not said, 'You shall not covet'. But sin, seizing an opportunity in the commandment, produced in me all kinds of covetousness. Apart from the law, sin lies dead. I was once alive apart from the law, but when the commandment came, sin revived and I died, and the very commandment that promised life proved to be death to me. For sin, seizing an opportunity in the commandment, deceived me and through it killed me. So the law is holy, and the commandment is holy and just and good. (Rom 7:7-12)

Paul did not speak here of the faith of Christ, but of his obedience. However, faith – in the sense of fidelity – can also be expressed as obedience. The change of language can be accounted for by the need to contrast Adam (disobedience) with Christ (obedience). 'Obedience' needs to be read in the light of *Romans 3:21-26*, as offered below in an adjusted version of the NRSV translation:

faith
obedience

> But now, apart from law, the righteousness of God has been disclosed, and is attested by the law and the prophets, the righteousness of God through the faith/fidelity of Jesus Christ for all who believe. For there is no distinction, since all have sinned and fall short of the glory of God; they are now justified by his grace as a gift, through the redemption that is in Christ Jesus, whom God put forward as a sacrifice of atonement by his blood, effective through [his] faith. He did this to show his righteousness, because in his divine forbearance he had passed over the sins previously committed; it was to prove at the present time that he himself is righteous and that he justifies the one who live from the faith/fidelity of Jesus. (Rom 3:21-26)

UNIT SEVEN
SECTION FOUR

4. CONCLUSIONS

Paul's main purpose here was not to develop what later tradition would regard as a full theology of Original Sin. Rather, his purpose in 5:12-21, as indeed in all of *Romans* 5-8, was to proclaim Christ and what took place for us in him. The language used for the Christ event here is especially important: gift, grace, justification/righteousness, life, righteous, eternal life.

The triumph of grace may be laid out as follows:

Adam	Christ
Trespass	Obedience
Condemnation	Justification
Death	Life

The presenting issue of *Romans* is still in Paul's mind, that is, the attitudes of superiority among Jews and gentiles. In *Romans* 1-4, Paul notes that there can be no distinction in practice on the basis of moral achievement. In *Romans* 5, he notes that there can be no distinction in principle, because of Adam's sin and because all have sinned. Lastly, in *Romans* 5-8, there can be no distinction on the basis of gift, because all have received indiscriminately and superabundantly from God in Christ. With such rich and deep salvation in common, how can there be any attitude of one looking down upon the other? The carefully chosen words, opening this moment in the discussion, can now be appreciated.

All have received indiscriminately and superabundantly from God in Christ.

> Therefore, since we are justified by [the] faith [fidelity of Christ], we have peace with God through our Lord Jesus Christ, … God's love has been poured into our hearts through the Holy Spirit that has been given to us. (Rom 4:1,3)

EXERCISE 5:

a) *Describe Paul's teaching on Adam in* Romans 5:12-21. *Write 5 lines.*

b) *Describe Paul's teaching on Jesus in* Romans 5:12-21. *Write 5 lines.*

SECTION FIVE:
ROMANS 9-11

Fig. 29: *The Jewish catacombs of Rome*

1.   INTRODUCTION

The next part of *Romans* is both passionate and dense. It touches on questions which arose much earlier in the letter – 'then what advantage has the Jew?' (Rom 3:1). The relationship between the Christian way and the mother religion is of concern across the whole New Testament, notably in the gospels and in Hebrews, and, of course, in Paul himself. It may help to remember that at the time of Paul we cannot yet speak of two religions, as the decisive break had not yet occurred. At this stage, the Christian way was one offshoot of Judaism, still struggling with its identity. Later in the first century there was far more antagonism between the mother religion and Christianity. It is not too much to say that *Romans* 9-11 constitutes the most complete direct treatment of this topic in the New Testament. It remains a corner-stone of Jewish-Christian relations today because of the assertion in those chapters that the early covenants have not been withdrawn.

> As regards the gospel they are enemies of God for your sake; but as regards election they are beloved, for the sake of their ancestors; *for the gifts and the calling of God are irrevocable.* (Rom 11:28-30)

Given the disastrous history of the Christian treatment of Jews, ending in the catastrophe of the *Shoah,* or Holocaust, *Romans* 9-11 assumes a greater importance because it deals *theologically* with the continuities and discontinuities between Judaism and Christianity. The big question behind the anguish and the argument is the consistency of God: 'I ask, then, has God rejected his people?' (Rom 11:1). This is precisely a theological question about the reliability of God; and as a person who believes in a God who can be trusted, Paul struggled to see the continuity amidst the more apparent discontinuity with Judaism. But the issue was not only theological, but also deeply personal. The opening verses of chapter 9 make that abundantly clear.

> I am speaking the truth in Christ – I am not lying; my conscience confirms it by the Holy Spirit – I have great sorrow and unceasing anguish in my heart. For I could wish that I myself were accursed and cut off from Christ for the sake of my own people, my kindred according to the flesh. They are Israelites, and to them belong the adoption, the glory, the covenants, the giving of the law, the worship, and the promises; to them belong the patriarchs, and from them, according to the flesh, comes the Messiah, who is over all, God blessed forever. Amen. (Rom 9:1-5)

As Paul was dealing here with a tragedy – the non-recognition by the chosen people of God's messiah – it may help to recall just how one deals with dark experiences in one's own life. In the past, when people faced some tragic loss, the frame within which it was seen was the classical worldview: everything that happens was seen as God's will. This put the believer in an impossible bind. To deal with the tragic loss, they could only go to God who, apparently, willed the loss in the first place. This is a static worldview, one which was the classical one for much of Christian history, including for Paul himself. Perhaps today there is another, less mechanistic view of what happens in time. Today, it is possible to think of the world-order under God being marked by a kind of randomness. We could call it 'ordered randomness' or 'random order'. In effect, this is the answer given by God in Job 38-39. Being able to see beyond the immediate darkness is something which Paul knew from his own experience.

> I want you to know, beloved, that what has happened to me has actually helped to spread the gospel, so that it has become known throughout the whole imperial guard and to everyone else that my imprisonment is for Christ; and most of the brothers and sisters, having been made confident in the Lord by my imprisonment, dare to speak the word with greater boldness and without fear. (Phil 1:12-14)

A more evolutionary world-view, allowing for that randomness without which there would be no evolution at all, permits us in today's language to think of God allowing but not willing tragedies. In a pastoral setting, this means that by acknowledging the suffering, there is no need to think of God as willing it, and it ought, at least, to make it easier in faith for the believer to turn to God.

More could be said, of course, because one is dealing here with 'the only question', that is, how to square faith in a good and just God with the fact of evil and innocent suffering. Perhaps, however, enough has been said to name the challenge facing Paul in these chapters. The eventual answer that will be given is in the classical mode, along the lines that God somehow willed what happened so that salvation would be extended to non-Jews. He doesn't really allow for random evolution and choice. However, one has to hear him, first, in his own voice.

2. PLACE IN THE ARGUMENT

This section shows the usual marks of a unit of argument in Paul.

2.1 VOCABULARY

The vocabulary at the beginning and the end touches the theme of descent from Abraham and the use of a remnant to save the whole people.

> It is not as though the word of God had failed. For not all *Israelites* truly belong to *Israel*, and not all of Abraham's children are his true descendants; but 'It is through *Isaac* that *descendants* shall be named for you.' This means that it is not the *children* of the flesh who are the *children* of God, but the *children* of the promise are counted as *descendants*. (Rom 9:6-8)

> I myself am an *Israelite*, a *descendant* of *Abraham*, a member of the tribe of *Benjamin*. (Rom 11:1)

Between these references, Paul mentions Sarah, Jacob, Esau, Moses, Abraham,

Hosea, Benjamin, Elijah, and the Israelite. We could include as well Rebecca and Isaac, and also David. It is quite a parade of Old Testament figures.

An important idea, though not hugely present in the vocabulary, is that of the remnant. Behind it lies a recollection of a pattern that is surprisingly present in the Bible. It begins in the pre-history with Noah, who was a kind of survivor and saving remnant. The most significant example is, however, the exile in Babylon when a few remained faithful and became the seed-corn for the replanting of God's people in the Holy Land. Paul used this idea of the saving remnant to say that the few Israelites/Jews who did recognise God's messiah when he came, can again be the seed-corn for the redemption of all Israel.

remnant

> And Isaiah cries out concerning Israel, 'Though the number of the children of Israel were like the sand of the sea, only a *remnant* of them will be saved'. (Rom 9:27)

> And as Isaiah predicted, 'If the Lord of hosts had not left *survivors* to us, we would have fared like Sodom and been made like Gomorrah.' (Rom 9:29)

> So too at the present time there is a *remnant*, chosen by grace. (Rom 11:5)

> But if *some of the branches* were broken off, and you, a wild olive shoot, were grafted in their place to share the rich root of the olive tree. (Rom 11:17)

> For if you have been cut from what is by nature a wild olive tree and grafted, contrary to nature, into a cultivated olive tree, how much more will these *natural branches be grafted back into their own olive tree.* (Rom 11:24)

2.2   FRAMES

Romans 9-11 is relatively easily marked off by two sets of frames or inclusions:

They are Israelites, and to them belong the adoption, the glory, the covenants, the giving of the law, the worship, and the promises; (Rom 9:4)	'And this is my covenant with them, when I take away their sins.' (Rom 11:27)
… to them belong the patriarchs, and from them, according to the flesh, comes the Messiah, who is over all, God blessed forever. Amen. (Rom 9:5)	For from him and through him and to him are all things. To him be the glory forever. Amen. (Rom 11:36)

2.3   RIVETS

As usual, towards the end of one block of arguments, Paul begins to anticipate some of the new argument to come.

Romans 9-11	Romans 12:1-15:6
So that *you may not claim to be wiser than you are, brothers and sisters*, I want you to understand this mystery: a hardening has come upon part of Israel, until the full number of the Gentiles has come in. (Rom 11:25) Just as you were once disobedient to God but have now received mercy because of their disobedience, so they have now been disobedient in order that, by the *mercy* shown to you, they too may now receive *mercy*. (Rom 11:30-31) For from him and through him and to him are all things. To him be the glory *forever* [lit. age]. Amen. (Rom 11:36)	I appeal to you therefore, *brothers and sisters*, by the *mercies* of God, to present your bodies as a living sacrifice, holy and acceptable to God, which is your spiritual worship. Do not be conformed to this *world* (lit. *age*) but be transformed by the renewing of your minds, so that you may discern what is the will of God – what is good and acceptable and perfect. For by the grace given to me I say to everyone among you *not to think of yourself more highly than you ought to think*, but to think with sober judgment, each according to the measure of faith that God has assigned. (Rom 12:1-3)

EXERCISE 6:

a) *Why did the relationship with the Jews matter so much to Paul? Write 5 lines.*

b) *Describe the delimitation of* Romans 9-11. *Write 5 lines.*

2.4   THESIS

Finally, Paul was coming around again to an important part of the original thesis of the letter.

> For I am not ashamed of the gospel; it is the power of God for salvation to everyone who has faith, to the Jew first and also to the Greek. For in it the righteousness of God is revealed through faith for faith; as it is written, 'The one who is righteous will live by faith.' (Rom 1:16-17)

The key questions are echoed in certain texts in these chapters. Paul is going to ask if the word of God has failed (9:6). Of course, this is unthinkable and he looks for patterns in the past to see how the present can be understood. The place of the Law in relationship to Christ stands at the centre of the topic (10:4). Paul argues by 'word place' here: Christ is the end of the Law. As in modern English, the Greek word for end, *telos*, carries the meanings of both goal and finish. Christ as the goal / end of the Law suggests continuity. Christ as the goal / finish of the Law suggests discontinuity. Finally, Paul asks the question again directly, 'I ask, then, has God rejected his people?' (Rom 11:1)

This can be summarised as follows:

Verses	Vocabulary	Frames	Rivers
Rom 9-11	Family descent and remnant	Covenants + Forever. Amen	Mercies, brothers and sisters, not to be wiser/ think of yourselves more highly, age (forever and world).
	Mostly in 9 and 11.	9:4-5	11:25, 30-31, 36 12:1-3
	Remnant, survivor, branches, olive tree	11:27, 36	

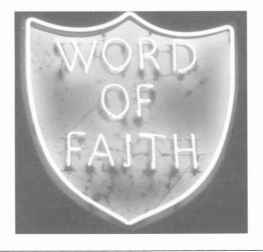

2.5 PROOF 3

In terms of the rhetoric, this brings on the third proof.

Verses	Letter	Rhetoric	Topic
1:1-7	Superscript		Sender, addressees and greetings
1:8-15/16-17	Thanksgiving	Introduction	Why Paul comes to Rome
1:16-17		Thesis	Justification and faith
1:18-4:23	Body	Proof 1	Jews and Gentiles in need
5:1-8:39		Proof 2	Jews and Gentiles in grace
9:1-11:36		Proof 3	Jews and Gentiles in God's plan
12:1-15:6		Proof 4	Jews and Gentiles living together
15:7-33		Conclusion	Why Paul comes to Rome
16:1-27	Postscript		Greeting to Roman Christians

2.6 THE STEPS IN THE ARGUMENT

Another way of mapping the text is to emphasise how Paul uses a concentric pattern to shape the overall argument.

Introduction	9:1-5	Enigma	
A Proof	9:6-29		God is consistent
B Proof	9:30-10:21		Torah v. Christ
A* Proof	11:1-32		God has a purpose
Conclusion	11:33-36	Mystery God's will	

3. ROMANS 9:6-29

After the impassioned introduction of 9:1-5, Paul argues for the consistency of God from a number of points of view. He does not fall into the trap of thinking that he has a complete rational explanation of everything. Instead, he selects a few key biblical ideas and uses them to find some pattern from the past. The topic remains the same: How it is that God seems to have lifted up the gentiles to such an extent that they outnumber those of God's chosen people?

3.1 THE REVERSAL OF PRIMOGENITURE

The *Book of Genesis* comes back again and again to the 'reversal of primogeniture'. For example, Abel was preferred to Cain, Jacob to Esau, Ephraim to Manasseh. This might seem unimportant until one asks the question: Why did the early Israelites tell themselves stories in which one brother without rights was promoted to the higher position? In part, it reflected their own sense of being puny in the region, very often the victims of imperial expansion, apparently insignificant and without power. Yet God chose Israel and promoted Israel, that is, God elected them to become his people. It was very penetrating of Paul to remind the Jews of this aspect of their identity as he showed them that they had formerly been insignificant in the very same way that the gentiles were insignificant now. God elected them to be his people as well. The argument has a subtle logic: if God could do this before, and you rejoiced in it, then God can do it again, and let us rejoice in it.

It is not as though the word of God had failed. For not all Israelites truly belonged to Israel, and not all of Abraham's children are his true descendants.

reversal of primogeniture

UNIT SEVEN SECTION FIVE

But 'It is through Isaac that descendants shall be named for you.' This means that it is not the children of the flesh that are the children of God, but the children of the promise who are counted as descendants. For this is what the promise said: 'About this time I will return and Sarah shall have a son.' Nor is that all; something similar happened to Rebecca when she conceived children by one husband, our ancestor Isaac. Even before they had been born or had done anything good or bad (so that God's purpose of election might continue, not by works but by his call), she was told, 'The elder shall serve the younger.' As it is written, 'I have loved Jacob, but I have hated Esau'. (Rom 9:6-13)

At this point in salvation history, God elevated the younger, that is the gentiles, in order to fulfil the promise to Abraham.

Paul had this argument before – both in *Galatians* and earlier in *Romans*. At this point in salvation history, God elevated the younger, that is the gentiles, in order to fulfil the promise to Abraham.

3.2   GOD'S SOVEREIGN WILL

The second argument is a very delicate one because it could destabilise God's justice and appear to favour a view of God's will as being arbitrary. It is part of God's identity to call whom he will. Probably no believer will wish to deny God his sovereign will, but the risk, of course, is the possibility of there being a capricious God. Paul, therefore, proceeded very carefully. When he illustrated, by a quotation, God's freedom, he echoed the name of God ('I am who I am'), and secondly he emphasised God's will as an expression of God's mercy and compassion, which is hard to stand against.

Paul expands this theme in an important way when he mentioned Pharaoh. In the book of Exodus, it is explained that God hardened the heart of Pharaoh so that the liberation of the people would be all the more powerful and glorious when eventually it happened. Jews at the time of Paul were comfortable with the idea that God could use a refusal of his glory for his own ends. But a mere idea might be insufficient for us; but it would have been accepted faithfully, and even perhaps gleefully, by the readers of the Book, but still found insufficient.

God was able to use the refusal of the majority of Jews for his own greater glory .

At this point in the argument, this is just an illustration, but it lays down some very important ground for Paul's core assertion in these chapters: God was able to use the refusal of the majority of Jews for his own greater glory by opening up salvation to the gentiles. This was a tough proposition, but Paul was working in a classical religious vein. Whatever happens must be in accordance with God's will. One would say today that God left people free and was able to use the negative reaction to Jesus as a way of including gentiles who would from then on become his chosen people.

God's injustice?

What then can one say? Is there injustice on God's part? By no means! For he says to Moses, 'I will have mercy on whom I have mercy, and I will have compassion on whom I have compassion'. So it depends, not on human will or exertion, but on God who shows mercy. For in the scriptures God says to Pharaoh, 'I have raised you up for the very purpose of showing my power in you, so that my name may be proclaimed in all the earth. So, then, God has mercy on whomever he chooses, and he hardens the heart of whomever he chooses. (Rom 9:14-18)

3.3   THE INSCRUTABILITY OF GOD'S WILL

Paul was always logical, and he realised that he may have here proved too much. If God acts like that, why should human beings bother at all, because he does what he wants to do anyway? The route out of this dilemma is the affirmation that God's will is beyond us. Again, this would not have been a foreign idea to Paul's hearers. Anyone of any maturity of faith has come to realise the utter mystery before which the human race stands.

God's will is beyond us.

> You will say to me then, 'Why then does he still find fault? For who can resist his will?' But who indeed are you, a human being, to argue with God? Will what is moulded say to the one who moulds it, 'Why have you made me like this?' Has the potter no right over the clay, to make out of the same lump one object for special use and another for ordinary use? (Rom 9:19-21)

He quotes here from the Bible the common image that God – the creator – is the potter, and we – humans from the *humus* of the earth – are the clay in his hands. While this inscrutability leaves the believer without a full understanding, it may be that the nearest one ever gets to a full understanding is that one must live without a full understanding!

One must live without a full understanding!

3.4   THE ROLE OF THE REMNANT

The final argument is rather more tangible. As noted above, another theme of the Hebrew Bible is that God has in the past saved and redeemed his people by a remnant, the handful of faithful Israelites who become the seed-corn of the next generation of believers. The most developed theology of the remnant comes from the time of the exile in Babylon. They needed some such theology because their kingdom was long destroyed and their religious centre, Jerusalem and its Temple, were no more. All the signs were that God had indeed abandoned his people. The prophets brought to the deportees the idea of a remnant, an idea designed to strengthen and galvanise the faithful so that when the time to return arrived, they would be ready, and more than ready.

All the signs were that God had indeed abandoned his people.

> On that day the remnant of Israel and the survivors of the house of Jacob will no more lean on the one who struck them, but will lean on the Lord, the Holy One of Israel, in truth. A remnant will return, the remnant of Jacob, to the mighty God. For though your people Israel were like the sand of the sea, only a remnant of them will return. Destruction is decreed, overflowing with righteousness. (Is 10:20-22)

> Then I myself will gather the remnant of my flock out of all the lands where I have driven them, and I will bring them back to their fold, and they shall be fruitful and multiply. (Jer 23:3)

This theology had served the people of Israel before, and it could serve them again. In effect, Paul states, it does not matter that only a few believed in Jesus, because this phenomenon had happened before and is consistent with previous experience.

What if God, desiring to show his wrath and to make known his power, has endured with much patience the objects of wrath that are made for destruction; and what if he has done so in order to make known the riches of his glory for the objects of mercy, which he has prepared
> beforehand for glory – including us whom he has called, not from the Jews only but also from the gentiles? As indeed he says in Hosea, 'Those who were not my people I will call "my people", and her who was not beloved I will call "beloved".' 'And in the very place where it was said to them, "You are not my people", there they shall be called children of the living God.' And Isaiah cries out concerning Israel, 'Though the number of the children of Israel were like the sand of the sea, only a remnant of them will be saved; for the Lord will execute his sentence on the earth quickly and decisively.' And as Isaiah predicted, 'If the Lord of hosts had not left survivors to us, we would have fared like Sodom and been made like Gomorrah.' (Rom 9:22-29)

The use of quotations from the Old Testament is very powerful here, and Paul displays his thorough knowledge of the text. He selects powerful passages written by Jews for Jews to uphold his understanding of the remnant – that is, the handful of true believers in Jesus.

4.   ROMANS 9:30-10:21

4.1   A KIND OF REVERSAL

At this point, Paul returned to an argument about faith and law, familiar from *Galatians* and from *Romans* 1-4. It is vital to recall that for Paul here, 'the law' means the ritual law, that is, the system of regulations which set Israel apart from other nations. Faith, as was seen in *Romans* 1-4, is best read as the faith of Christ, that is, the 'bridge relationship' put in place by God to enable believers to be justified, to be in right relationship with God. By means of this bridge relationship, it was possible to live the moral law. Finally, because of Jesus' solidarity with all 'outside the blessing', there was no place any longer for a separated people of God.

bridge relationship

There was no place any longer for a separated people of God.

> For there is no distinction between Jew and Greek; the same Lord is Lord of all and is generous to all who call on him. For, 'Everyone who calls on the name of the Lord shall be saved'. (Rom 10:12-13)

It is noticeable that the number of citations increases here. Paul is assessing the behaviour of Israel, but not simply as a matter of his own opinion but through the lens of scripture. The very last line is both judgment and appeal:

> But I ask, have they not heard? Indeed they have; for 'Their voice has gone out to all the earth, and their words to the ends of the world'. Again I ask, did Israel not understand? First Moses says, 'I will make you jealous of those who are not a nation; with a foolish nation I will make you angry'. Then Isaiah is so bold as to say, 'I have been found by those who did not seek me; I have shown myself to those who did not ask for me'. But of Israel he says, 'All day long I have held out my hands to a disobedient and contrary people'. (Rom 10:18-21)

4.2   END, GOAL AND FULFILMENT

The second section here (verses 5-13) puts the importance of the faith, not only of Christ but also of the believer, clearly in place.

> … because if you confess with your lips that Jesus is Lord and believe in your heart that God raised him from the dead, you will be saved. For one believes with the heart and so is justified, and one confesses with the mouth and so is saved. (Rom 10:9-11)

> So faith comes from what is heard, and what is heard comes through the word of Christ. (Rom 10:17)

EXERCISE 7:

a) *Describe any one of the arguments lined up by Paul in* Romans *9:6-29. Write 5 lines.*

b) *Describe the theological place of* Romans 9-11 *in* Romans *as a whole. Write 5 lines.*

5.   ROMANS 11:1-32

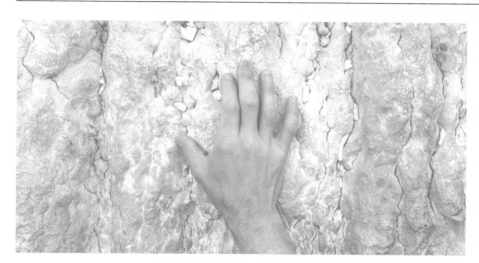

In this section Paul returns to the theme of the destiny of Israel and that of the gentiles.

5.1   A REMNANT KEPT FAITH

In *Romans* 11:1-6, Paul applies his theology of the remnant. The offer of salvation – initially rejected and then opened to the gentiles – is still on offer, and God has not rejected his people. This remnant is not identified by the works of the ritual law, but by grace, because the remnant has experienced and believed in what God did for humanity in Christ.

5.2   ARGUMENTS FROM SCRIPTURE

Paul uses a quotation which seems to have been used right across the New Testament, to account for the rejection of Jesus by most Jews.

> Make the mind of this people dull, and stop their ears, and shut their eyes, so that they may not look with their eyes, and listen with their ears, and comprehend with their minds, and turn and be healed. (Is 6:10)

Matthew	Mark	Luke
With them indeed is fulfilled the prophecy of Isaiah that says: 'You will indeed listen, but never understand, and you will indeed look, but never perceive'. (Matthew 13:14)	In order that 'they may indeed look, but not perceive, and may indeed listen, but not understand; so that they may not turn again and be forgiven.' (Mark 4:12)	He said, 'To you it has been given to know the secrets of the kingdom of God; but to others I speak in parables, so that 'looking they may not perceive, and listening they may not understand.' (Luke 8:10)
Acts	**Romans**	**John**
Go to this people and say, You will indeed listen, but never understand, and you will indeed look, but never perceive. (Acts 28:26)	As it is written, 'God gave them a sluggish spirit, eyes that would not see and ears that would not hear, down to this very day.' (Romans 11:8)	He has blinded their eyes and hardened their heart, so that they might not look with their eyes, and understand with their heart and turn – and I would heal them. (John 12:40)

Many scholars would agree that the purpose in each of the above uses of the text is similar. In each context, although in different ways, the writers / speakers were dealing with the mystery of Israel's rejection of the Messiah. Because they lived in the classical world-view, they could incorporate this negative perspective into God's plan only by putting it down to God's inscrutable will. Paul concludes the passage with a very warm *a fortiori* argument: given that their rejection produced so much good, how much more good would their inclusion produce?

God's inscrutable will?

5.3   THE OLIVE TREE

At this point, with so much emphasis on the failure and disobedience of the Jews, it could be that the gentiles began to feel puffed up. To counter such a feeling of superiority, Paul addressed them directly and challenged them with a remarkable metaphor.

> Now I am speaking to you Gentiles. Inasmuch then as I am an apostle to the gentiles, I glorify my ministry in order to make my own people jealous, and thus save some of them. For if their rejection is the reconciliation of the world, what will their acceptance be but life from the dead! If the part of the dough offered as first fruits is holy, then the whole batch is holy; and if the root is holy, then the branches also are holy. (Rom 11:13-16)

Then, in a passage which is worth reading very carefully, he explained about the olive tree:

> But if some of the branches were broken off, and you, a wild olive shoot, were grafted in their place to share the rich root of the olive tree, do not boast over the branches. If you do boast, remember that it is not you that supports the root, but the root that supports you. You will say, 'Branches were broken off so that I might be grafted in.' That is true. They were broken off because of their unbelief, but you stand only through faith. So do not become proud, but stand in awe. For if God did not spare the natural branches, perhaps he will not spare you. Note then the kindness and the severity of God: severity toward those who have fallen, but God's kindness toward you, provided you continue in his kindness; otherwise you also will be cut off. And even those of Israel, if they do not persist in unbelief, will be grafted in, for God has the power to graft them in again. For if you have been cut from what is by nature a wild olive tree and grafted, contrary to nature, into a cultivated olive tree, how much more will these natural branches be grafted back into their own olive tree. (Rom 11:17-24)

Students will not have missed the note of threat: *for if God did not spare the natural branches, perhaps he will not spare you.* All the same, that is not the tone of the passage as a whole. As a whole it is affirmative and really expresses in another way the message of the whole letter that there is no distinction between Jew and Greek.

Paul then concluded this pained and hopeful teaching with a summary, and then, as always, a citation to bolster the teaching.

> So that you may not claim to be wiser than you are, brothers and sisters, I want you to understand this mystery: a hardening has come upon part of Israel, until the full number of the gentiles has come in. And so all Israel will be saved; as it is written, 'Out of Zion will come the Deliverer; he will banish ungodliness from Jacob'. 'And this is my covenant with them, when I take away their sins'. (Rom 11:25-27)

To balance the judgement delivered here, Paul added a reminder to all, and to the gentiles in particular, that all are incapable before God; as was seen in *Romans 1-4.*

> For God has imprisoned all in disobedience so that he may be merciful to all. (Rom 11:32)

6.   CONCLUSION

The very last part of the argument echoes the beginning. Paul started, in *Romans 9:1-5,* with the great enigma, and concluded here with that even greater enigma – the mind of God himself (11:33-36). In some sense, it means that even though the previous arguments were penetrating and brilliant, at another level, there remains an unknown and perhaps an unknowable dimension to it all. Paul rises to great poetry.

There remains an unknown and perhaps an unknowable dimension to it all.

> O the depth of the riches and wisdom and knowledge of God! How unsearchable are his judgments and how inscrutable his ways! 'For who has known the mind of the Lord? Or who has been his counsellor?' 'Or who has given a gift to him, to receive a gift in return?' For from him and through him and to him are all things. To him be the glory forever. Amen. (Rom 11:33-36)

There is much to reflect upon here. Today, there is a flourishing dialogue between Jews and Christians. At its heart stands the teaching of Paul that the promises were never withdrawn. The rootedness of Christianity in Judaism is marked most Sundays with a reading from the Old Testament, not to mention the Jewishness of the liturgy as a whole.

The rootedness of Christianity in Judaism is marked every Sunday with a reading from the Old Testament.

Everyone has experienced the mystery of refusal, the negative, and yet in spite of that, God can 'write straight with our crooked lines'. And a continuing part of the journey of faith is a faith in God's unseen purpose, not only in the grand events of the world, but in one's own life. One should not plunge too soon into the mystery, but all the same, there is an irreducible enigma in spite of all the human capacity for rationality and intellection.

EXERCISE 8:

a) *Describe the image of the olive tree in* Romans 11. *Write 5 lines.*

b) *Describe Paul's understanding, in* Romans 11, *of the future of Judaism. Write 5 lines.*

SECTION SIX:
ROMANS 12:1-15:6

I. INTRODUCTION

The next part of *Romans* (Rom 12:1-15:6) is both passionate and dense.

At last, Paul gets around to the practical advice which he hoped would help the Roman Christians resolve the tension in their community. The principles behind this advice have been expounded at length in chapters 1-11, and now the practice is brought to the fore.

The advice given here could be of use at both micro and macro level in church life today. At micro level, it is common to experience tensions, different theologies and various pieties, and a lack of tolerance. At the macro level, there is in St Paul a tremendous resource for ecumenical dialogue, hitherto neglected. In particular, Paul proposed 'a tolerance of difference' which can be content to agree on the central issues, and leave other matters to individual practice and need. The Second Vatican Council echoed this discernment when it spoke of the hierarchy of doctrine, indicating that not every teaching is at the same level. In the Reformed tradition, the question of whether something is 'church dividing' or not is also a reception of Paul's teaching. In a word, there is much here that can speak to Christians today, as individuals and as members of believing communities.

This text will now be examined as a unity.

a tolerance of difference

hierarchy of doctrine

2.   DELIMITATION

2.1   VOCABULARY

The vocabulary of 12:1-15:6 is marked by the language of mutuality and mutual belonging. The image of the body is foundational (v.12) and Paul builds on that by speaking of one's neighbour, oneself, and brothers and sisters. It is couched in the language of imperatives, and it comes to a close in 15:6.

mutuality

2.2   FRAMES

The beginning and the end resemble each other. One should notice that the words 'appeal' and 'encouragement' have the same root in Greek. Corresponding to 'worship', Paul writes: 'together you may with one voice glorify the God and Father of our Lord Jesus Christ'.

I **appeal** to you therefore, brothers and sisters, by the mercies of **God**, to present your bodies as a **living** sacrifice, holy and acceptable to God, which is your spiritual **worship**. Do not be conformed to this world, but be transformed by the renewing of your minds, *so that you may* discern what is the will of **God** – what is good and acceptable and perfect. (Rom 12:1-2)	May the **God** of steadfastness and **encouragement** grant you to **live** in harmony with one another, in accordance with Christ Jesus, *so that* together *you may* with one voice **glorify** the **God** and Father of our Lord Jesus Christ. (Rom 15:5-6)

2.3   RIVETS

There is bridge vocabulary and bridge thought right across the close of chapter 11 and the opening of chapter 12:

So that you may not ***claim to be wiser*** than you are, brothers and sisters, I want you to understand this mystery: a hardening has come upon part of Israel, until the full number of the Gentiles has come in. Just as you were once disobedient to God but have now received **mercy** because of their disobedience, so they have now been disobedient in order that, by the **mercy** shown to you, they too may now receive **mercy**. 'For who has known the **mind** of the Lord? Or who has been his counsellor?' (Rom 11:25,30-31,34)	I appeal to you therefore, brothers and sisters, by the **mercies** of God, to present your bodies as a living sacrifice, holy and acceptable to God, which is your spiritual worship. Do not be conformed to this world, but be transformed by the renewing of your **minds**, so that you may discern what is the will of God – what is good and acceptable and perfect. For by the grace given to me I say to everyone among you not ***to think of yourself more highly*** than you ought to think, but to think with sober judgment, each according to the measure of faith that God has assigned. (Rom 12:1-3)

Similarly, there is a match between the close of 15:5-6 and the continuation in 15:7-8:

May the **God** of steadfastness and encouragement grant you to live in harmony with **one another**, in accordance with Christ Jesus, so that together you may with one voice *glorify* the God and Father of our Lord Jesus **Christ**. (Rom 15:5-6)	Welcome **one another**, therefore, just as **Christ** has welcomed you, for the *glory* of **God**. (Rom 15:7-8)

Noticing these apparently technical details provides a good indication of what the unit itself is dealing with.

2.4   STRUCTURE

Within the overall persuasion of *Romans*, this passage relates to the other units as follows:

Rom 1-4	Rom 5-8	Rom 9-11	Rom 12:1-15:6
No distinction	A large family	No Distinction	Welcome others
Inclusion of Jew and gentile		Inclusion of Israel	Live inclusively!

The discussion, starting in 12:1, has the following sequence:

a)   Christian life as 'reasonable worship' (12:1-2)

b)   What does Christian living require? (12:3-13:14)
  i.   Your own gifts (12:3-8)
  ii. Gift of love within the community (12:9-16)
  iii. Love in action outside the community (12:17-21)
  iv. How should Christians treat civil authorities? (13:1-7)
  v.   Being indebted in love (13:8-10)
  vi. Knowing the time (13:11-14)

c)   Living inclusively and in tolerance of each other (14:1-15:6)
  i.   Tolerance is the call of everyone (14:1-12)
  ii. The strong, especially, should be tolerant of the weak (14:13-23)
  iii. The example of Jesus, who was himself so tolerant (15:1-6)

All the steps would be interesting to investigate, but because of limits of space, this study will confine itself to the third section above, 14:1-15:6. Behind this important practical section stands the image of the body of Christ as underpinning the counsel given.

3.   ROMANS 14:1-15:6

At this point, students are invited to read the passage carefully and ask questions before going on to the text below.

3.1   TOLERANCE IS THE CALL
Romans 14:1-12

> ¹Welcome those who are weak in faith, but not for the purpose of quarrelling over opinions. ²Some believe in eating anything, while the weak eat only vegetables. ³Those who eat must not despise those who abstain, and those who abstain must not pass judgment on those who eat; for God has welcomed them. ⁴Who are you to pass judgment on the servants of another? It is before their own lord that they stand or fall. And they will be upheld, for the Lord is able to make them stand. (Rom 14:1-4)
>
> ⁵Some judge one day to be better than another, while others judge all days to be alike. Let all be fully convinced in their own minds. ⁶Those who observe the day, observe it in honour of the Lord. Also those who eat, eat in honour of the Lord, since they give thanks to God; while those who abstain, abstain in honour of the Lord and give thanks to God. (Rom 14:5-6)
>
> ⁷We do not live to ourselves, and we do not die to ourselves. ⁸If we live, we live to the Lord, and if we die, we die to the Lord; so then, whether we live or whether we die, we are the Lord's. ⁹For to this end Christ died and lived again, so that he might be Lord of both the dead and the living. (Rom 14:7-9)

¹⁰Why do you pass judgment on your brother or sister? Or you, why do you despise your brother or sister? For we will all stand before the judgment seat of God. ¹¹For it is written,

'As I live, says the Lord, every knee shall bow to me,
and every tongue shall give praise to God.'

¹²So then, each of us will be accountable to God. (Rom 14:10-12)

Who are the weak and who are the strong? It is likely that the weak are those who abstain from meat sacrificed to idols or at the very least observe the dietary laws very strictly. As was seen in Corinth, food left over from pagan sacrifices was sold, and often it was the only way for poor people to afford meat. The weak were also probably observing the Sabbath. This practice was regarded by Romans as a sign of laziness among the Jews. Paul's argument has several layers.

- First of all, it is not the place of believers to assess each other and pass judgment on each other (vv. 3-4). Paul returns to that topic in verses 10-12, this time using Scripture for support.

- The second argument is that we should do everything for the honour of the Lord and not, he implies, for the shame of a brother or sister.

- The third argument is that Christ died for us so that we could share his resurrected life and, he implies, not so that we could avoid food or mark holy days. Christians are engaged in something so much greater and should not be quarrelling over this or that practice.

3.2 THE STRONG AND THE WEAK

Romans 14:13-23

¹³Let us therefore no longer pass judgment on one another, but resolve instead never to put a stumbling block or hindrance in the way of another. ¹⁴I know and am persuaded in the Lord Jesus that nothing is unclean in itself; but it is unclean for anyone who thinks it unclean. ¹⁵If your brother or sister is being injured by what you eat, you are no longer walking in love. Do not let what you eat cause the ruin of one for whom Christ died. ¹⁶So do not let your good be spoken of as evil. ¹⁷For the kingdom of God is not food and drink but righteousness and peace and joy in the Holy Spirit. ¹⁸The one who thus serves Christ is acceptable to God and has human approval. ¹⁹Let us then pursue what makes for peace and for mutual upbuilding. ²⁰Do not, for the sake of food, destroy the work of God. Everything is indeed clean, but it is wrong for you to make others fall by what you eat; ²¹it is good not to eat meat or drink wine or do anything that makes your brother or sister stumble. ²²The faith that you have, have as your own conviction before God. Blessed are those who have no reason to condemn themselves because of what they approve. ²³But those who have doubts are condemned if they eat, because they do not act from faith; for whatever does not proceed from faith is sin. (Rom 14:13-23)

In the light of verses 1-12, Paul then gave his opinion. He knew that no food is clean or unclean (v.14 and v.20), so in one sense he is with the strong. The Kingdom of God is not about such things. Nevertheless, he identified a greater responsibility for those who are strong or more mature. A flaunted freedom and, even worse, the despising of those who lack it, would be contrary to the principle of love and would fail to promote peace and mutual upbuilding.

Thus Paul calls on a greater generosity of spirit among the mature. One could wonder if the same principle might not have applied to Peter in Galatians 2:11-14. However, the principle is also not so easy to apply because it gives the ruling hand to those who are less grown up and less free in themselves. Nevertheless, the principle stands that the building up of the body of Christ is more important than the optional exercise of freedom.

3.3   THE EXAMPLE OF JESUS

Romans 15:1-6

¹We who are strong ought to put up with the failings of the weak, and not to please ourselves. ²Each of us must please our neighbour for the good purpose of building up the neighbour. ³For Christ did not please himself; but, as it is written, 'The insults of those who insult you have fallen on me'. ⁴For whatever was written in former days was written for our instruction, so that by steadfastness and by the encouragement of the scriptures we might have hope. ⁵May the God of steadfastness and encouragement grant you to live in harmony with one another, in accordance with Christ Jesus, ⁶so that together you may with one voice glorify the God and Father of our Lord Jesus Christ. (Rom 15:1-6)

At this point the mask of impartiality slips slightly and Paul declares his hand: 'we who are strong'. From a persuasion point of view, he might lose the weak at this point because he identifies himself clearly with the other party. At the same time, the use of 'we' is designed to signal to the strong that in one sense they really are right. But the full verse is an appeal: We who are strong ought to put up with the failings of the weak, and not to please ourselves. The great example given here is Jesus himself. Within a faith discourse, there can be no higher appeal because all agree that Jesus 'did not please himself'. Finally, he exhorts them to live in harmony in order that their worship may be truly a communion, offered with one voice. Thus at the end of 12:1-15:6, he brings his readers / hearers back to the starting point of reasonable worship, proper humility and the body of Christ:

> I appeal to you therefore, brothers and sisters, by the mercies of God, to present your bodies as a living sacrifice, holy and acceptable to God, which is your spiritual worship. Do not be conformed to this world, but be transformed by the renewing of your minds, so that you may discern what is the will of God – what is good and acceptable and perfect. For by the grace given to me I say to everyone among you not to think of yourself more highly than you ought to think, but to think with sober judgment, each according to the measure of faith that God has assigned. For as in one body we have many members, and not all the members have the same function, so we, who are many, are one body in Christ, and individually we are members one of another. (Rom 12:1-6)

4.   CONCLUSION

Romans 12:1-15:6 covers a wide range of topics about living. Nowhere is it more pertinent to the Roman communities than in chapter 14. There Paul developed important principles for mutual tolerance and respect. Very properly, he demanded a higher generosity from those who were more advanced in faith. They too ought not lose sight of the example of Christ and the greater good of the body of believers. This, perhaps neglected, reasoning of Paul has potential today for all kinds of situations both macro and micro. The macro would include the big issues of churches coming together as the fruit of the ecumenical movement. As Christians await that moment, Paul himself would want us to focus on the micro, to do what we need to do to promote harmony and tolerance so that our worship might truly be a communion.

EXERCISE 9:

a) Describe the 'weak' and the 'strong' in Romans 14. Write 5 lines.

b) Describe Paul's practical theology of tolerance. Write 5 lines.

SECTION SEVEN:
THE END AND THE BEGINNING

Romans 15:7-33

1.   INTRODUCTION

Anyone who has ever made a presentation knows the importance of the conclusion. In the conclusion, the speaker must think again about the audience – what has been learned and how are they feeling – and only then construct the end. In particular, it is important to summarise what has been said without seeming to repeat it. It is also important to connect again with the audience and even to touch their feelings at this late stage because emotional memory lasts longer. Drawing together the strands of the persuasion may well determine the success of the project as a whole. Accordingly, Paul devotes special care to the close of the *Letter to the Romans*.

For the last time, the delimitation of the text must be examined first.

2.   DELIMITATION

2.1   VOCABULARY

It will be seen in detail below that Paul uses two sets of vocabulary in 15:7-33. The first set, in verses 7-12, summarises the argument as a whole, and the second set, in verses 13-33, uses flashback vocabulary, taking the reader back to the very beginning of the letter.

2.2   FRAMES

This time the frame is somewhat weaker.

a)   Both verses suggest worship;

b)   both 'welcome one another' and 'peace' promote the mutuality which is the topic of the letter; and

c)   God is mentioned in both.

Welcome one another, therefore, just as Christ has welcomed you, for the glory of God. (Rom 15:7)	The God of peace be with all of you. Amen. (Rom 15:33)

Given the relative weakness of the frames, the vocabulary and the rivets assume a greater importance.

2.3   RIVETS

The links which enable the shift from the final proof to the conclusion are clear:

[5]May the God of steadfastness and encouragement grant you to live in harmony with **one another**, in accordance with **Christ** Jesus, [6]so that together you may with one voice **glorify** the **God** and Father of our Lord Jesus Christ. (Rom 15:5-6)	Welcome **one another**, therefore, just as **Christ** has welcomed you, for the **glory** of **God**. (Rom 15:7)

There is no need for a rivet between 15 and 16, because 16 clearly belongs to the letter *genre* as Paul initiates an important sequence of greetings.

2.4   STRUCTURE

At this point, the document divides into two parts. The first part is the summary of the letter, found in verses 7-12, and the second part recalls the start, found in verses 8-33.

3.   CONCLUSION AND THESIS RELATED

Romans 15:7-12 and 1:16-17

The main task of the conclusion is to summarise what has gone before. In *Romans* 15:7-9 (with the following citations as support) Paul achieved one of his most succinct and power statements.

> [7]Welcome one another, therefore, just as Christ has welcomed you, for the glory of God. [8]For I tell you that Christ has become a servant of the circumcised on behalf of the truth of God in order that he might confirm the promises given to the patriarchs, [9]and in order that the Gentiles might glorify God for his mercy. (Rom 15:7-9)

3.1   VOCABULARY

Students will notice how each expression picks up on important words used earlier in the letter.

7:    Therefore welcome (14:1,3), one another (1:12,27; 2:15; 12:5,10,16; 13:8; 14:13,19; 15:5) as Christ has welcome you for the glory (1:23; 2:7,10; 3:7,23; 4:20; 5:2;6:4; 8:18,21; 9:4,23; 11:36) of God.

8:    I say that Christ has become (1:3, 2:25; 3:19; 4:18;6;5; 7:3-4; 9:29; 10:20; 11:5-6,9,17,25,34; 12:16) a servant (13:4) of the circumcised (2:25-3:1; 3:30; 4:9-12) for the sake of the truth (1:18,25; 2:2,8,20; 3:7; 9:1) of God in order to fulfill the promises (4:13-14,16,20; 9:4,8-9) of the fathers (4:11-12,16-18; 9:5,10; 11:28)

9:    so that the gentiles (1:5,13; 2:14,24; 3:29; 4:17-18; 9:24,30; 10:19; 11:11-13,25) might glorify (1:21; 8:30; 11:13; 15:6) God for his mercy (9:23; 11:21)

3.2   FUNCTION

It is not only the words which reflect the whole letter, but the ideas of the letter are found here in their entirety.

12-15 = ⁷Welcome one another, therefore, just as Christ has welcomed you, for the glory of God.	9-11 = in order that he might confirm the promises given to the patriarchs,
1-4 = ⁸For I tell you that Christ has become a servant of the circumcised on behalf of the truth of God	5-8 = ⁹and in order that the Gentiles might glorify God for his mercy.

This tight summary of the whole letter corresponds to 1:16-17. Those brief verses are truly the seedcorn of the entire persuasion in *Romans*.

Romans 1:16-17	Chapters	Romans 15:7-9
Power of God for salvation	5-8: justification, salvation	*⁹and in order that the Gentiles might glorify God for his mercy.*
Everyone who has faith	1-4 Justification, faith	*⁸For I tell you that Christ has become a servant of the circumcised on behalf of the truth of God*
to the Jew first and the then to the Greek	9-11 Israelites and Gentiles	*in order that he might confirm the promises given to the patriarchs,*
The one who is righteous will live by faith	12-15 Living together in faith the gift of saving justification	*⁷Welcome one another, therefore, just as Christ has welcomed you, for the glory of God.*

In Paul, the word of God has a powerful confirmatory purpose, and so it is here.

Romans 15:9*b*-12

> ⁹ᵇAs it is written,
>> 'Therefore I will confess you among the gentiles,
>>> and sing praises to your name';
>
> ¹⁰and again he says,
>> 'Rejoice, O gentiles, with his people';
>
> ¹¹and again,
>> 'Praise the Lord, all you gentiles,
>>> and let all the peoples praise him';
>
> ¹²and again Isaiah says,
>> 'The root of Jesse shall come,
>>> the one who rises to rule the gentiles;
>> in him the gentiles shall hope'.

4.   CONCLUSION II AND INTRODUCTION RELATED

Romans 15:13-33 and 1:8-17

It is a natural thing for speakers at the end of a speech to echo something of the beginning. While this is not an object of explicit reflection in the rhetorical handbooks of the period, it is a distinctive feature of Paul's writings. Thus, in *Romans* 15:13-33 there is a distinct recalling of 1:8-17. For the hearer / reader, a kind of flashback over the whole persuasion is triggered.

Romans 1:8-17	**Romans 15:13-33**
1:8 First, I thank my God through Jesus Christ for all of you, because **your faith** is proclaimed throughout the world.	*15:14* I myself feel confident about you, my brothers and sisters, that you yourselves are full of **goodness**, filled with all **knowledge**, and able to **instruct** one another.
⁹For **God**, whom I serve with my **spirit** by announcing the gospel of his Son, is my witness that without ceasing I remember you always in my **prayers**, ¹⁰asking that by **God's** will I may somehow at last succeed in coming to you.	*15:30* I appeal to you, brothers and sisters, by our Lord Jesus Christ and by the love of the **Spirit**, to join me in earnest **prayer** to **God** on my behalf,
¹¹For I am longing to see you so that I may share with you some spiritual gift to **strengthen** you – ¹²or rather so that we may be **mutually encouraged** by **each other's** faith, both yours and mine.	*15:32* so that by God's will I may come to you with **joy** and be **refreshed** in your **company**.
¹³I want you to know, brothers and sisters, that I have often intended to **come** to you (but thus far have been prevented), in order that I may reap some harvest among you as I have among the rest of the Gentiles.	*15:22* This is the reason that I have so often been hindered from **coming** to you.
1:14 I am a debtor both to **Greeks** and to barbarians, both to the wise and to the foolish – ¹⁵hence my eagerness to **proclaim** the **gospel** to you also who are in **Rome**.	*15:18* For I will not venture to speak of anything except what Christ has accomplished through me to win obedience from the **Gentiles**, by word and deed, 19 by the power of signs and wonders, by the power of the Spirit of God, so that from **Jerusalem** and as far around as **Illyricum** I have fully **proclaimed** the **good news** of Christ.

Finally, Paul closes this whole appeal with a very human admission of weakness and frailty:

> I appeal to you, brothers and sisters, by our Lord Jesus Christ and by the love of the Spirit, to join me in earnest prayer to God on my behalf, that I may be rescued from the unbelievers in Judea, and that my ministry to Jerusalem may be acceptable to the saints, so that by God's will I may come to you with joy and be refreshed in your company. The God of peace be with all of you. Amen. (Rom 15:30-33)

The Roman Christians must have been moved by Paul's anxiety about Jerusalem and longing for Rome. In this rather technical analysis, one has seen that Paul fulfils perfectly the functions of the conclusion: to summarise, to get the good will of his audience, and to move them on his behalf. It might even be possible to schematise the various aspects thus:

Functions of the conclusion:

summing up (*enumeratio*)	=	Rom 15:7-9.10-13
amplification (*amplificatio*)	=	Rom 15:14-29
and appeal to pity = (*commiseratio*)		Rom 15:30-33

5. GREETINGS AT THE START OF ROMANS

Only now is it possible to appreciate the subtlety and depth of the very first verses of this letter. Students should take a moment to ponder these verses now.

> Paul, a servant of Jesus Christ, called to be an apostle, set apart for the gospel of God, which he promised beforehand through his prophets in the holy scriptures, the gospel concerning his Son, who was descended from David according to the flesh and was declared to be Son of God with power according to the spirit of holiness by resurrection from the dead, Jesus Christ our Lord, through whom we have received grace and apostleship to bring about the obedience of faith among all the Gentiles for the sake of his name, including yourselves who are called to belong to Jesus Christ, to all God's beloved in Rome, who are called to be saints: Grace to you and peace from God our Father and the Lord Jesus Christ. (Rom 1:1-7)

Again, there is here a kind of summary in anticipation.

1	Paul,	
		a servant of **Jesus Christ**,
		called to be an **apostle**,
		set apart for the gospel of **God**,
2		**which** he promised beforehand through his prophets
		in the *holy* scriptures,
3		**concerning** his Son,
		who **was descended**
		from David
		according to the flesh
4		and **was declared** to be **Son** of **God** with power
		according to the spirit of *holiness*
		from [by] resurrection from the dead,
		<u>**Jesus Christ**</u> our **Lord**,
5		**through whom**
		we have received grace and **apostleship**
		to bring about the obedience of faith among **all** the Gentiles
		for the sake of his name,
6		including yourselves who are **called** to belong to <u>**Jesus Christ**</u>,
7		To **all God's** beloved in Rome,
		who are **called** to be *holy ones*:
		Grace to you and peace from **God** our Father
		and the **Lord** <u>**Jesus Christ**</u>.

It would have been possible to have written a much shorter introductory greeting, perhaps including verses 1 and 7. However, Paul chose to insert a compressed synthesis of what he was going to say to the Roman communities. He would be working closely from scripture (v.2) to show that the Jews have a priority in salvation (v.3) but that this salvation has been opened to the gentiles by the resurrection of Jesus (v.4), and that Paul himself now has a special role to these very gentiles (vv.5-6). At the opening of *Romans* a reader might perhaps have overlooked the careful planting of ideas which would grow into mighty theological arguments as the letter unfolds.

EXERCISE 10:

a) *What are the parallels between Romans 1:8-17 and 15:13-33? Write 5 lines.*

b) *What is the theology embedded in the greeting of the letter, Romans 1: 1-7. Write 5 lines.*

UNIT SEVEN CONCLUSIONS

Fig. 30: *Roman Pantheon Oculus*

I.   THE PROCLAMATION OF JESUS CHRIST

Romans is one of the great Christians documents.

Romans 16 is, from a church point of view, a subversive document because it names so many women as evangelists, deacons and apostles.

Any brief summary – except one by Paul himself – is bound to be an injustice to the *Letter to the Romans*. *Romans* is one of the great Christian documents, perhaps the greatest that Paul himself produced. It is perhaps easier to read than *Galatians* but it is still a difficult read. Clearly Paul trusts the letter bearer – perhaps Phoebe – and indeed the Romans to grasp the deep theology and the practical advice. The letter comes to rest with a wonderful series of greetings. *Romans* 16 is, from a church point of view, a subversive document because it names so many women as evangelists, deacons and apostles. The prayer at the end can serve to close this introduction to the study of *Romans*.

> Now to God who is able to strengthen you according to my gospel and the proclamation of Jesus Christ, according to the revelation of the mystery that was kept secret for long ages but is now disclosed, and through the prophetic writings is made known to all the Gentiles, according to the command of the eternal God, to bring about the obedience of faith – to the only wise God, through Jesus Christ, to whom be the glory forever! Amen. (Rom 16:25-27)

2. LEARNING OUTCOMES ASSESSED

By the end of this unit, in addition to the learning outcomes listed at the beginning, students should have:

a)   a basic grasp of how Christianity arrived in Rome;

b)   a picture of the history of the Christian movement in Rome;

c)   an understanding of why Paul wrote to the Roman communities;

d)   a fundamental idea of the overall argument and lay-out of the letter;

e)   an appreciation *Romans* 1:16-4:25 – all in need before God;

f)   a sense of what unites Jews and gentiles in *Romans* 5-8;

g)   an initial grasp of the ideas in *Romans* 9-11 – the relationship of Jews and Christians;

h)   an appreciation 'of the potential for today' of Paul's practical theology of tolerance in *Romans* 12:1-15:6;

i)   a literary appreciation of the introduction and conclusion to the argument in *Romans* 1:8-16 and 15:7-33; and

j)   an understanding of the subtle anticipation of the theology the whole letter as outlined in *Romans* 1:1-7.

MODULE CONCLUSIONS

1.   CHARACTERISTICS OF PAUL

Sometimes people wonder what St Paul looked like. He is known somewhat from the painting tradition which is remarkably consistent – or conservative – over many centuries. The earliest known portrait of Paul seems to be the one found in the Catacombs of St Thecla, on the Via Ostiense in Rome. It is a serious portrait, with a furrowed brow and a receding hairline. Later in the tradition, he acquired a sword as a symbol of the word of God,

> Indeed, the word of God is living and active, sharper than any two-edged sword, piercing until it divides soul from spirit, joints from marrow; it is able to judge the thoughts and intentions of the heart. (Heb 4:12)

There exists, however, a quite early verbal description of Paul. This occurs in the *Acts of Paul and Thecla*, a work dating from the second half of the second century. In the *Acts of Paul and Thecla*, one finds traditions and legends about Paul's missionary activity. In particular, his association with a young woman called Thecla finds expression in a series of episodes. In general, scholars would doubt the usefulness of the *Acts* with respect to the missionary activity of the historical Paul. Rather, this document, which is very interesting in itself, reveals something of the second century attitudes towards asceticism, religious enthusiasm and credulity. Nevertheless, it does contain a purported description of the apostle Paul, as follows:

> A certain man, by name Onesiphorus, hearing that Paul had come to Iconium, went out to meet him with his children Silas and Zeno, and his wife Lectra, in order that he might entertain him: for Titus had informed him what Paul was like in appearance: for he had not seen him in the flesh, but only in the spirit. He went along the road to Lystra, and stood waiting for him, and kept looking at the passers by according to the description of Titus. He saw Paul coming, a man small in size, bald-headed, bandy-legged, well-built, with eyebrows meeting, rather long-nosed, full of grace. For sometimes he seemed like a man, and sometimes he had the countenance of an angel.
>
> (*Acts of Paul and Thecla*:1:3)

Sometimes this is taken to be historical because it is not seen as flattering. However, the value of such descriptions becomes apparent only when one realises that each feature had at the time a conventional interpretation. Pliny, in his *Natural History*, wrote:

> When the forehead is large it indicates that the mind beneath it is sluggish; people with a small forehead have a nimble mind, those with a round forehead an irascible mind ...
>
> When people's eyebrows are level this signifies that they are gentle, when they are curved at the side of the nose, they are stern, when bent down at the temples that they are mockers, when entirely drooping, that they are malevolent and spiteful.
>
> If people's eyes are narrow on both sides, this shows them to be malicious in character; eyes that have fleshy corners on the side of the nostrils show a mark of maliciousness; when the white part of the eyes is extensive, it conveys an indication if impudence; eyes that have a habit of repeatedly closing indicate unreliability.
>
> Large ears are a sign of talkativeness and silliness.
>
> (Pliny: *Natural History*, 11.275-6)

So, in brief, the description can be decoded as follows:

> Small in stature: that is, nimble, lively because the blood has a short trip around the body;
>
> Bald-headed: a mark of humanity, as distinct from animal.
>
> Bandy-legged: grounded, earthed, realistic.
>
> Well-built: energetic.
>
> Eyebrows meeting: gentle.
>
> Long-nosed: of royal or noble lineage.
>
> Full of grace: the gift from God which shaped Paul.

In a word, under the guise of a description of the outer person, a summary of the inner person has been furnished. If one leaves aside the appearance and look only at the interpretation, it turns out that the interpretation is not at all wide of the mark. Paul was indeed amazingly nimble, certainly in mind, probably also in body. He comes across as being very human indeed, with a highly realistic and grounded appraisal of the world and its inhabitants. While he could be fierce, his desire was to be gentle, which he mostly was. The tribe of Benjamin was no mean lineage; a hint of family nobility alerts one to the astonishing nobility of spirit exhibited in the letters. And surely, he was graced by God, full of grace, a receiver of grace and a gracious giver of all he had himself received.

2.   KNOWLEDGE OF CHRIST

This study has encountered a passionate visionary through the seven undisputed letters. Throughout his relatively long life, he was always a man of faith and energy, before and after his 'turning'. His mind was penetrating – never taking issues on the surface but thinking deeply about the real issues at stake. He loved his communities and respected them enough to always give them his most profound, sometimes difficult, theology. He was a man of prayer, whose relationship to Christ was there for all to see, even when he was being cautious about special religious experiences. His physical energy, the immense journeys, the suffering, the joys, all speak of someone on fire, incandescent with the Good News. Paul, the earliest theologian of the New Testament, may very well have been also the greatest. He truly became what he proclaimed, so that he could say without fear of contradiction or even a hint of boasting: 'imitate me'. Even at the end of his life, he lifted us up with his humanity, his courage, his faith and his vision.

> Not that I have already obtained this or have already reached the goal; but I press on to make it my own, because Christ Jesus has made me his own. Beloved, I do not consider that I have made it my own; but this one thing I do: forgetting what lies behind and straining forward to what lies ahead, I press on toward the goal for the prize of the heavenly call of God in Christ Jesus (Phil 3:12-15)

3.   LEARNING OUTCOMES ASSESSED

By the end of this module, in addition to the learning outcomes listed at the very beginning of the module, students should have:

a)   a grasp of Paul's theology of grace;

b)   an understanding of Paul's theology of redemption;

c)   an appreciation of the social and theological function of the Lord's Supper in the Pauline churches;

d)   the ability to describe the social setting and community membership in the Christian communities addressed;

e)   a knowledge of Paul's teaching on freedom; and

f)   a sense of the growing divisions between Jews and gentiles in the Christian church, and between Christians and the secular powers.

BIBLIOGRAPHY

General Works

The New Jerome Biblical Commentary, Fitzmyer, J.A., Brown, R.E. and Murphy, R.E. (eds.), 1990 London, Geoffrey Chapman/Prentice-Hall.

Commentaries

Ascough Richard S., Cotton, Sandy: *Passionate Visionary – Leadership Lessons from the Apostle Paul*, 2005, Toronton, Novalis.

Barrett, C.K. Paul: *An Introduction to his Thought*, 1994, London, Geoffrey Chapmann.

Brown, Raymond: *Introduction to the New Testament*, Anchor Bible Reference Library, 1997, New York and London, Doubleday.

Bornkamm, Günther: *Paul*, 1985, London, Hodder and Stoughton.

Branick, Vincent: *The House Church in the Writings of Paul*, 1989, Wilmington, Michael Glazier.

Brisebois, Mireille: *St Paul – Introduction to St Paul and his Letters*, 1986, Middlegreen, St Paul Publication.

Campbell, William S.: *Paul and the Creation of Christian Identity*, 2006, London/New York, T&T Clark.

Dunn, James D.G.: *The Cambridge Companion to St Paul*, 2003, Cambridge, CUP.

Gaventa, Beverly Roberts: *Our Mother Saint Paul*, 2007, Louisville/London, Westminster John Knox Press.

Gorman, Michael: *Reading Paul*, 2008, Milton Keynes, Paternoster.

Harrington, Daniel J.: *Meeting St Paul Today – Understanding the Man, His Mission, and His Message*, 2008, Chicago, Loyola Press.

Hengel, Martin: *The Pre-Christian Paul*, 1991, London, SCM.

Hooker, Morna D.: *Paul – A Short Introduction*, 2003, Oxford, Oneworld.

Horrell, D.: *An Introduction to the Study of Paul* (Continuum Biblical Studies Series), 2000, London, Continuum.

Martyn, J.Louis: *Galatians*, 1997, New York, Doubleday.

Matera, Frank: *Strategies for Preaching St Paul*, 2001, Collegeville, The Liturgical Press.

Matera, Frank: *New Testament Christology*, 1999, Louisville, Westminster/John Knox.

O'Mahony, Kieran J.: *Do We Still Need St Paul? A Contemporary Reading of the Apostle*, 2009, Dublin, Veritas.

Puskas, Charles B.: *The Letters of Paul – An Introduction*, 1993, Collegeville, The Liturgical Press.

Roetzel, Calvin: *Paul – A Jew on the Margins*, 2003, Louiseville, Westminster John Knox Press.

Sanders, E. P.: *Paul*, 1991, Oxford, OUP.

Still, Todd D. (ed.): *Jesus and Paul Reconnected – Fresh Pathways into an Old Debate*, 2007, Grand Rapids, Eerdmans.

Witherup, Ronald D.: *101 Question & Answers on Paul*, 2003, New York, Paulist.

Wright, N.T.: *Paul in Fresh Perspective*, 2005, Minneapolis, Fortress.

—   *What St Paul Really Said – Was Paul of Tarsus the Real Founder of Christianity?* 1997, Oxford, Lion.

Ziesler, J.: *Pauline Christianity*, 1990 (rev. ed.), Oxford, OUP.

Short Bibliography on Letters in Antiquity

Aune, David E.: *The New Testament in Its Literary Environment*, 1988, Cambridge, James Clarke & Company.

Bailey, James L. and Vander-Broek, Lyle D.: *Literary Forms in the New Testament*, 1992, London, SPCK.

Doty, W.G.: *Letters in Primitive Christianity*, 1973/1988 (5th printing), Philadelphia, Fortress Press.

Malherbe, A.J.: *Ancient Epistolary Theorists*, SBL Sources for Biblical Study 19, 1988, Atlanta, Scholars Press.

Murphy-O'Connor, J.: *Paul the Letter-Writer – His World, His Options, His Skills*, 1995, Collegeville, MN, The Liturgical Press.

Stirewalt, M. Luther.: *Paul the Letter Writer*, 2003, Grand Rapids, Eerdmans.

Stowers, Stanley K.: 'Letters (Greek and Latin)' in ABD IV, 290-293.

A Short Bibliography on Rhetoric

Anderson, R. Dean: *Ancient Rhetorical Theory and Paul*, 1996, Kampen, Kok Pharos.

Aune, David E.: *The Westminster Dictionary of New Testament and Early Christian Literature & Rhetoric*, 2003, Louiseville/London, Westminster John Knox Press.

Kennedy, George A.: *A New History of Classical Rhetoric*, 1994, Princeton, Princeton University Press.

Kennedy, George A.: *New Testament Interpretation through Rhetorical Criticism*, 1984, Chapel Hill and London, University of North Carolina Press.

— *The Art of Persuasion in Greece*, 1963, London, Routledge & Keegan Paul.

— *The Art of Rhetoric in the Roman World*, 1972, Princeton, Princeton University Press.

Mack, Burton: *Rhetoric and the New Testament*, 1990, Minneapolis, Fortress.

Wilder, A.: *Early Christian Rhetoric*, 1971, Peabody, Hendrickson.

1 Thessalonians

Malherbe, Abraham: *The Letters to the Thessalonians*, 2000, Doubleday, New York.

Murphy-O'Connor, J.: *Paul the Letter-Writer – His World, His Options, His Skills*, 1995, Collegeville, MN, The Liturgical Press.

O'Mahony, K.: 'The Rhetorical Dispositio of 1 Thessalonians', in PIBA 25 (2002), pp.81-96.

Donfried, Karl P. and Marshall, I. Howard: 'The Theology of 1 Thessalonians', in *The Theology of the Shorter Pauline Letters*, 1999 , Cambridge, CUP, ch.1.

UNIT FOUR FURTHER READING

Philemon

Dunn, James G.D.: *The Epistles to the Colossians and to Philemon – A Commentary on the Greek Text*, New International Greek Testament Commentary), 2006, Grand Rapids, Eerdmans.

Fitzmyer, Joseph: *The Letter to Philemon*, 2000, Yale, Yale University Press.

Thurston, Bonnie B. and Ryan, Judith: *Philippians and Philemon*, Sacra Pagina Series, 2009, Collegeville, The Liturgical Press.

UNIT FIVE FURTHER READING

Philippians

Fee, Gordan D.: *Paul's Letter to the Philippians – A Commentary on the Greek Text*, New International Greek Testament Commentary, 1995, Grand Rapids, Eerdmans.

O'Brien, Peter T.: *The Epistle to the Philippians – A Commentary on the Greek Text*, New International Greek Testament Commentary, 1991, Grand Rapids, Eerdmans.

Reumann, John: *Philippians*, 2008, Yale, Yale University Press.

UNIT SIX FURTHER READING

1 Corinthians

Collins, Raymond, Harrington, Daniel J., First Corinthians, Sacra Pagina Series, Collegeville: The Liturgical Press, 2007.

Fee, Gordan D., The First Epistle to the Corinthians. A Commentary on the Greek Text (New International Greek Testament Commentary) Grand Rapids: Eerdmans, 1987.

Fitzmyer, Joseph, First Corinthians, Yale: Yale University Press, 2008.

Mitchel, Margaret M., Paul and the Rhetoric of Reconciliation: An Exegetical Investigation of the Language and Composition of 1 Corinthians Louisville: Westminster/John Knox, 1991

Murphy O'Connor, Jerome: *St Paul's Corinth*, 3rd revised and expanded edition, 2002, Collegeville, Liturgical Press.

Witherington III, Ben: *Conflict & Community in Corinth – A Socio-Rhetorical Commentary on 1 and 2 Corinthians*, 1995, Grand Rapids, Eerdmans.

2 Corinthians

Barnett, Paul: *The Second Epistle to the Corinthians – A Commentary on the Greek Text*, New International Greek Testament Commentary, 1997, Grand Rapids, Eerdmans.

Danker, Frederick W.: *2 Corinthians*, 1989, Minneapolis (MN), Augsburg Publishing House.

Kreitzer, Larry: 'Paul and the Jerusalem Collection', chapter 6 of *2 Corinthians*, 1996, Sheffield, Sheffield Academic Press.

Lambrecht, Jan: *Second Corinthians*, Sacra Pagina Series, 2007, Collegeville, The Liturgical Press.

UNIT SEVEN FURTHER READING

Romans

Barrett, C.K.: *The Epistle to the Romans*, 1987, London, A and C Black (first published, 1957).

Byrne, Brendan: *Romans*, Sacra Pagina Series, 2007, Collegeville, The Liturgical Press.

Donfried, Karl P. and Richardson, Peter (eds.): *Judaism and Christianity in First-Century Rome*, 1998, Grand Rapids, Eerdmans.

Elliot, Neill: *The Rhetoric of Romans*, 2007, Minneapolis, Fortress.

Fitzmyer, Joseph: *Romans*, 1993, New York, Anchor Bible Edition.

Lampe, Peter: *From Paul to Valentinus – Christians at Rome in the First Two Centuries*, 2003, Minneapolis, Fortress.

Moo, Douglas: *The Epistle to the Romans – A Commentary on the Greek Text*, New International Greek Testament Commentary, 1996, Grand Rapids, Eerdmans.

Morgan, R.: *Romans*, New Testament Guides, 1997, Sheffield, Sheffield Academic Press.

 # ERRATUM

On page 19 of Volume One of this module, the final sentence should read:

'In fact, a sense of guilt is not an overriding theme of rabbinic literature.'

GLOSSARY

Alexandrinus: a codex of the Bible from the V century ce.

Amplificatio: the expansion of a passage, for emphasis and greater detail.

Apocalyptic: a Jewish worldview, which saw the end of the world coming, leading to a huge crisis, the final judgment and God's establishment of a just kingdom.

Captatio benevolentiae: a passage of writing designed to win or capture (*captatio*) the good will (*benvolentiae*) of the reader or listener, often by means of flattery.

Charis: the Greek word for gift or favour.

Claromontanus: a codex of the Bible from the V century ce.

Codex: a book, the opposite of a scroll; plural, codices.

Coherent: that general teaching of Paul, which lies behind his teaching in a particular context. See *Contingent*.

Compilation: the possibility that an ancient document as we now have it is a combination of two or more earlier ones.

Confirmatio: a proof, another word for probatio.

Contingent: that concrete aspect of Paul's teaching which is particular to a situation. See *Coherent*.

Covenantal nomism: the name given to Jewish religion in the light of the New Perspective. It means that the practice of the law (Greek: *nomos*) is a response to the Covenant and not a means of 'creating' grace.

Cynic: a popular philosophy, according to which the adherents practised radical detachment from material things, so as to enjoy inner freedom and peace.

Dead Sea Scrolls: documents found in the Judean desert from 1947 onwards which were in the library of a dissident Jewish community living on the shores of the Dead Sea.

Deliberative: a speech which promotes a policy, usually in a political settings.

Delimination: discovering the natural units of a text, using indicators in the text itself such as framing or rivets.

Deutero-Pauline: letters in Paul's name, which scholars often think are not by Paul. Examples would be 1 and 2 *Timothy, Titus, Ephesians* and *Colossians*.

Diatribe: addressing a fictional or real opponent in the course of a speech.

Display: a speech for a congratulatory occasion, for example a Roman Triumph.

Dispositio: the lay-out of a speech (Latin: *exordium, narratio, propositio, probation[es], peroratio*). Greek: *taxis*.

Elocutio: the decoration of a speech to make it sound beautiful. Greek: *lexis*.

Ephraemi Rescriptus: a codex of the Bible from the fifth century ce.

Epicureanism: a philosophy based on the teaching of Epicurus (c.371 bce-c.271 bce). It was a materialist approach, which advocated inner freedom through asceticism and detachment.

Epistolary: to do with letters and letter-writing.

Exhortation: an instruction, usually moral.

Exordium: the introduction to a speech. (Greek: *proimon*).

Forensic: a speech in a court, either prosecuting or defending.

Framing: the use of the same expression at the start and end of a segment of text.

Gezerah shavah: a biblical argument based on a two or more texts sharing the same word.

Hagadic: to do with the hagadah or stories of the Bible.

Halakhic: to do with the halakah or moral teaching of the Bible.

Hellenistic: Greek culture, after the time of Alexander the Great, especially outside of Greece.

Interpolation: the possibility that a section has been added or inserted into an earlier document.

Inventio: the 'discovery' of what needs to be said in a particular situation. (Greek: *euresis*).

Justification: right relationship with God, in a covenant context.

Kerygma: the proclamation of the Good News.

Memoria: the memorisation of a speech. (Greek: *mneme*).

Metaphysics: classical philosophy investigating the nature of reality, especially 'being' as such.

Midrash: a kind of ruminative expansion of a text, which can constitute an argument.

Mishnah: an early collection of rabbinic teachings.

Narratio: the statement of facts, essential in a court cast. (Greek: *diegesis*).

New Perspective: a current in Pauline studies initiated by E. P. Sanders.

Papyrus 30: a papyrus of the New Testament from about the third century ce.

Papyrus 46: a papyrus of the New Testament from about 200 ce.

Papyrus 51: a papyrus of the New Testament from about 400 ce.

Papyrus 61: a papyrus of the New Testament from about 700 ce.

Papyrus 65: a papyrus of the New Testament from about the third century ce

Papyrus: a kind of paper made of the papyrus reed.

Peroratio: the conclusion of a speech. Greek: *epilogos*.

Pistis: the Greek word of faith or trust.

Postscript: the final greeting in a letter.

Probatio: a proof; plural probationes.

Pronuntiatio: practising the performance of a speech. Greek: *hupokrasis*.

Propositio: the thesis or topic of a speech. Greek: *prothesis*.

Refutation: an argument against a position.

Rhetoric: the ancient science of preparing and delivering a speech.

Ritual Law: the identity marks of Judaism, that is, circumcision, the dietary laws and Sabbath observance.

Rivet: the use of the same expression at the end of one section and the beginning of the next section.

Septuagint: the ancient translation of the Hebrew Bible into Greek.

Sinaiticus: a codex of the Bible from the IV century ce.

Stoicism: a school of philosophy, whose founder was Zeno of Citium in the third century bce. They promoted inner freedom by an ascetical approach to the appetites.

Superscript: the introductory greeting in a letter.

Syntax: the grammatical structure of Greek sentences.

Talmud: a huge collection of rabbinic teaching, incorporating the Mishnah.

Torah: the Pentateuch or the Law, consisting of the first five books of the Bible.

Vaticanus: a codex of the Bible from the fourth century ce.